"My friend Jay Dennis has a great and tender heart for ministry at its elemental and most human levels. May God bless his important and abiding work. May the healing and help Jay is offering be providentially restorative."
— TIM GOEGLEIN, vice-president of external relations,
Focus on the Family

"Pornography is not a harmless addiction. It is often a root that leads to broken marriages, child abuse, and physical harm—leaving a trail of victims in its wake. Dr. Jay Dennis's Join 1 Million Men in the War Against Pornography is a wonderful ministry that seeks to set men (and women) free from the destruction of pornography. His heart for God and his desire to restore purity to men and women in the church drives Dr. Dennis's vision of Join 1 Million Men in the War Against Pornography. And his call for One Million Women Praying to see the church porn free is one that we gainfully support."
— SHARI RENDALL, director of legislation and public policy,
Concerned Women for America

"Pornography is a cancer, destroying lives and ruining families. Jay Dennis is a wise and careful surgeon, using the fine scalpel of God's Word to help men gain victory over this moral disease. It's my hope that fully 1 million men and even more will find hope and healing through this outstanding resource."
— ROBERT F. SCHWARZWALDER JR., senior vice-president,
Family Research Council

"I'm happy to endorse the Join 1 Million Men in the War Against Pornography project. Pornography is an epidemic that has paralyzed many men from moving forward in a walk with God, and from serving as church leaders. This aggressive project should raise the bar for countless men who have been caught in the web of pornography. By God's grace, it will help them find a Christ-centered repentance and transformation that will liberate and empower them, their families, and churches."
— RANDY ALCORN, author of The Purity Principle and Heaven

Our
Hardcore
Battle Plan
for Wives

Join 1 Million Men in the War Against Pornography Includes

Join1MillionMen.org

Our Hardcore Battle Plan A–Z

Our Hardcore Battle Plan App

Our Hardcore Battle Plan DVD

Our Hardcore Battle Plan Commitment

Our Hardcore Battle Plan: Joining in the War Against Pornography

Our Hardcore Battle Plan: 1 Million Women Praying

Our HARDCORE BATTLE PLAN *for Wives*

Winning in the War Against Pornography

JAY DENNIS & CATHY DYER

NEW HOPE
PUBLISHERS
Gospel-Centered. Missions-Driven.

BIRMINGHAM, ALABAMA

New Hope® Publishers
P. O. Box 12065
Birmingham, AL 35202-2065
NewHopeDigital.com
New Hope Publishers is a division of WMU®.

Library of Congress Control Number: 2013939277

Web site URLs provided accessed April 2013.
Cover design: Casscom
Interior design: Glynese Northam
Special thanks to Vicki Huffman and Gail Allyn Short

ISBN-10: 1-59669-371-1
ISBN-13: 978-1-59669-371-5

N134112 • 0613 • 4M1

JOIN
1 MILLION
MEN

JOIN1MILLIONMEN.ORG

To every wife who says, "We will win in the
war against pornography."

Cathy Dyer explains how her husband's secret addiction came to light, dramatically changing their lives forever—how it all exploded.

Table of Contents

Acknowledgments

Beyond my experiences with the needs at First Baptist Church at the Mall, I studied the facts about sexual addiction, in the process obtaining certification in sexual addictions through the Institute for Sexual Wholeness, Atlanta, Georgia.

Institute leadership—Dr. Michael Sytsma, Dr. Doug Rosenau, and Debra Taylor—were phenomenal examples of godliness and excellence in addressing a sensitive issue.

Dr. Mark Laaser, a pioneer in Christian sexual addiction issues, encouraged and helped me to learn even more. I am so grateful for him and his Faithful and True Ministries. The materials he writes along with his lovely wife, Debra, are excellent and useful.

Along the way, Craig Gross of XXXChurch has been very helpful in sharing wisdom and counsel. God is greatly using him.

Luke Gilkerson and the staff team at Covenant Eyes have been an incredible encouragement to me in this process and I cannot thank them enough for their counsel.

I want to thank Tanis Leo, a prayer warrior from Canada, who spoke words of encouragement and affirmation that this ministry could touch the world.

Thank you, Pastor Tim Osiowy and Gateway Christian Ministries in Prince George Island, British Columbia, for gathering around me and praying God's anointing and protection.

Thank you to so many others who are committed to this movement; as I travel, speak with, and work alongside you in this movement, I am grateful to see how God is using you for His glory.

A special thank you to Cathy and Greg Dyer, for your courage in sharing your success story—because of Christ. I know that it will be a blessing to many wives, couples, and their families. God bless you!

A special thank-you to what I believe is the greatest church on earth, First Baptist Church at the Mall, and the fantastic staff and people who are family. Thank you for believing in your pastor.

And now, to the most important acknowledgment of all, to my precious wife, Angie. You have shown incredible understanding, love, patience, encouragement, and have been the greatest prayer warrior to me and the best friend a man could ever have.

Mrs. Angie Dennis

Introduction

Editor's note: *Cathy Dyer's world was shaken to its core because of her husband's pornography addiction, affair, and later, his abandonment of her and her precious baby. Her testimony shows the depth of pain pornography can cause and the height of mercy, redemption, and healing that comes through repentance. Through telling her story and opening up the pages of her journal, she shows how her pain eventually turned to praise.*

FROM CATHY DYER:

Approximately seven years into my marriage, a crisis arose that nearly destroyed it. Then on May 7, 2013, my husband and I celebrated our 19th anniversary, which means we are now 12 years beyond that crisis. I was impressed yet again by the amazing, healing power of God. And now, because time has passed and because it really does heal many wounds, I feel I can finally reflect and write about my experience. I have shared with many individuals and groups about the experience my husband and I went through, but I have never put it down in writing, and it is time to do so. Writing has always been a way for me to deal with and reflect on occurrences in my life. I have kept diaries and written in journals since age ten, and it has always been a major part of how I understand the world and especially the people in my life.

When I went through my ordeal, it was the stories similar to my predicament that ministered to me the most and brought me solace and comfort. Of course, the most influential story to me was the life of Christ. No other individual has endured more pain, more rejection, more betrayal, and more human suffering than Jesus, and knowing that my Savior knew from experience the pain of betrayal and had complete empathy for my situation was more comforting than anyone's words ever could have been.

There is one more reason that I chose to write about this time in my family's life: our story is a testimony of God's ability to turn tragedy into triumph. He took what Satan meant for destruction and transformed it into an amazing story of the power of love and grace. As Scripture puts it, He changed our ashes into beauty (Isaiah 61:3 NIV). My simple hope is that others will be encouraged by what God has done in our lives.

> Editor's Note: *There is a reason you are reading this book. Maybe you are just interested in the subject or you have a friend who is dealing with the issue. Maybe you know or you suspect that someone in your life is struggling, or might struggle with the temptation to view pornography—or who has already given in to that temptation. If that describes you, hoping the problem will go away is not an option. With each passing day, the person who struggles will become more ensnared in this addiction. Jay Dennis knows this and has a deep passion to help free the multitudes of men (and women) who are struggling with an addiction to pornography. He has seen the devastation pornography can cause to marriages and families, and he knows that in every sense of the word, the struggle against it is a battle.*

FROM JAY DENNIS:

Let me share with you what happened at First Baptist Church at the Mall in Lakeland, Florida, the church I have been privileged to lead since February of 1996. As I was looking for materials to help our men in their struggle with pornography, I made some critical discoveries. There was good material written from parachurch organizations, from counselors, and from academics, however, I did not see the kind of material I needed to present that was written from the heart of a senior pastor. That is when God convicted me to learn all I could about the issue and write material that is truth-based and grace-driven, with boldness, yet understanding that this is a sensitive subject when dealing with it inside the walls of the church.

I attended the Institute for Sexual Wholeness in Atlanta, Georgia, and took the class portion for the certification in sexual addictions.

Once the material initially was written, I asked the men in our church to meet with me for six Wednesday evening sessions. I made the commitment to hold nothing back as it related to sexual issues and pornography. The response, honestly, surprised me. On the third week, during the conclusion of the teaching time, I asked our men to stand if they were struggling with pornography. The vast majority of the men (about 300) stood to their feet. I had my eyes closed and head bowed, but I could hear the sound of many theater seats hitting the backs of the chairs. I thought, *This sounds like the beginning of freedom.*

From that night, a spirit of revival broke out among our men; it was the beginning of a journey that continues to affect positively the men, marriages, and families of our church. I added an additional evening to speak only to the women. In addition, I asked our parents to come together as I shared a teaching on "Protecting Your Child from Sexual Brokenness."

I asked all the men of our church to make a commitment to live a pornography-free life. I felt it was important to encourage not only the men who were struggling with pornography to make the commitment, but also those who do not struggle. I told them to "draw a line in the sand to share with your family and friends that you are making a commitment to never go there!"

We gave out commitment cards where the part with each man's name was prominent and the other portion was kept for our records. We built a huge wall in the lobby of our church to display all the commitment cards from our men. We wanted wives, families, and other men in the church to see the obvious, public commitment they had made. At this writing, we have well over 1,000 men whose names are on the wall. The wall has become an opportunity for our church to discuss this sensitive issue. The door has been opened to demonstrate our men's passion for purity. This is something every church of any size and denomination can do.

Another part of our emphasis in the battle against pornography is called Join1MillionMen.org. The idea for it came in the midst of preparing materials for the men of my church. It was around Thanksgiving in 2009 and I was flying back from Fort Smith, Arkansas, after visiting with my mom who had lost her husband (my dad) earlier that year. While in a Christian bookstore there I picked up a book by John Maxwell called *Put Your Dream to the Test*. Reading it on the plane back to Tampa, I came across a statement that hit me like a ton of bricks, "If you don't quantify your dream, you will never be able to communicate it." The Holy Spirit clearly placed on my heart: "1 million men." Obviously that was exciting! Yet, what was the rest of that 1 million men? For the next two weeks my question to God was, But 1 million men . . . what? I sought Him and then He filled in the blank—1 Million Men Porn Free.

Now that we have quantified the dream, we want to communicate it. If churches of all sizes and denominations would get involved, we could have an army of men committed to purity, and that purity could bring a powerful awakening in churches! What can you do as a woman reading this book? You can be aware of the facts and feelings surrounding this issue for Christian men, women, families, and churches; adopt a biblical battle plan for yourself and your home; and commit to act in community to battle this evil. When godly women begin praying, God-sized things happen!

Part 1
The War

OUT OF NOWHERE, PART A

When a Woman's World Is Shaken

The year 2000 was, without a doubt, the year of the most extreme highs and lows I have ever experienced. My greatest high came in April, when my eldest daughter, Meghan, was born and my most heartbreaking low came when my husband of almost seven years left me and our three-month-old little girl. He announced it to me in the wee hours of July 19—2:00 A.M. to be exact. His words cut through my grogginess quite effectively as he told me he had an apartment in town and was leaving.

I was on summer break and didn't have to go back to work at the Christian school where I taught for another month. That month was eye-opening and confusing, heart-wrenching and raw. Literally, overnight, I learned that my husband was not only a porn addict but was also having an affair with a woman from work. I had to ask myself, *How did this happen to a man who not even a week before was a board member at our church and the head usher who greeted people as they came in the sanctuary doors?*

I felt tricked, betrayed, and stupid. *How had I missed the signs?* Life became a daily cry-fest of pain, heartbreak, anger, and loneliness. And in the midst of it all, I tried to care for my beautiful baby, who was so unaware of the emotional destruction around her. Caring for her kept me sane in those months after Greg left. She was one of God's bright spots in an otherwise joyless existence.

God was closer to me in those months than I have ever felt Him before. Psalm 34:18 (NIV) was my stronghold: "The Lord is close to the brokenhearted and saves those who are crushed in spirit." I can tell you with assurance that this verse is true—I lived it.

July 19, 2000

Shock. I had to remind myself to breathe—and not too quickly. Why was something so reflexive suddenly so difficult? My feet were frozen to the floor as I watched him walk out. I wanted to run after, shake, and maybe even slap him—anything to get him to realize the obvious mistake he was making. But all I could do was remain still and concentrate on each breath. I don't know how long I stood there, watching the door expectantly while some small part of my mind clung to the possibility of his return. Eventually, my brain figured it knew better. I willed my feet to move, walked out the front door to my porch, and sat down on the top step, utterly defeated.

It was about 2:00 A.M. Nothing stirred in our neighborhood, and the aloneness of the silence was deafening. Tears flowed freely from my eyes, but little sound escaped my lips. I struggled with the reality my mind was rejecting. *This couldn't be happening!* It was not what I wanted, and I certainly didn't deserve it. The thought kept surfacing that this was a horrific nightmare and, eventually, I would awaken, shaky and scared but warm in my bed.

After some time had passed and my mind began to accept instead of deny, the grim truth sank in: *my husband of nearly seven years just left me, and I have a precious three-month-old daughter sleeping blissfully unaware in her crib upstairs.* The more I dealt with this reality, the more I felt as if I were out of my body, looking down at something out of a soap opera . . . a really bad soap opera. I remember an insane-sounding giggle coming from my mouth, fighting its way out through the tears. I had the brief thought that I should call my mom and dad, or my brother and sister-in-law, who lived within walking distance. But my too-calm inner voice said, *no, don't wake them.* They, like my sleeping daughter, still lived in the world of Cathy and Greg. Now it was just Cathy. I didn't want to wake them with that harsh reality. It had been horrible enough for me to find out while I was half asleep. *Let them have a good night's sleep before they have to deal with the stark ugliness of this moment.*

I found out weeks later that during those first hours I was most likely in a medical state of shock. And I do remember fighting off a few bouts of hyperventilation. When I finally decided to go back inside, I had checked the time and was surprised to see that it was 4:00 A.M. *My baby girl will wake in an hour or two for her feeding.* Once that thought broke through the fog in my mind, the outright sobbing commenced.

I remember packing up Greg's things and finding hidden pornographic magazines. My brother found some others. In a spurt of honesty, Greg had admitted the pornography addiction that had spanned nearly half his life, and we both believe it was the root of his affair. I couldn't believe that this man I had known for more than ten years was not at all who I thought he was.

Life went on. While Greg lived a life of partying, drinking, and doing drugs, I raised our baby and went back to work. While he probably felt like he had a scarlet *A* on his chest, I felt like I had a scarlet *S* for "stupid" on mine. *How had I not seen this coming?*

8-27-00
Sunday

School starts tomorrow. I am scared.
Can I do this single mother thing?
God has been so near to me, and
yet I fear. Trusting is such a
hurdle. Trusting the outcome. It's
silly, really. I have a hard time
trusting THE ALMIGHTY to work
things out? Who am I that He
puts up with me?
At this point, I don't want Greg.
I feel he is lost, and I have been
so hurt... I just don't think I can
get past all he's done. I realize
God can work a miracle, but I
try not to raise hope.
I hurt so deeply — deeper than I
knew pain could reach. I am alone.
No human companion.
God, be my strength. Help me to see
you working and know that as crazy
as things seem, YOU ARE IN CONTROL.
I know I am not truly alone. you
are always here. Thank you.

Let your joy be my joy
Let your strength be my strength
Lord, fill me up with songs of praise
And I will praise your name/ And I
will lift my voice/ For your love for me
is great/ I REJOICE

9/30/00 I am ready for divorce.

> Saturday, 9-30
> I don't want to go to sleep tonight.
> I'm painfully aware of my aloneness.
> Some nights, exhaustion overtakes me
> before I can dwell on it; but most
> nights, I cry as it washes over me
> relentlessly. I pray that God will
> pass through these waters with me,
> just as He promised (Is. 43:2), but
> I also pray that He would cause
> this nightmare to end soon. I'm
> so ready to awaken! I sense His
> presence and am really grateful, but
> it's still so hard. What do I expect?
> It is DIVORCE — a severing of
> what was once one. How
> harsh! The realization never
> ceases to overwhelm me. You'd
> think after 2½ months, it
> would stop shocking me. But
> betrayal is a fierce animal
> that kills slowly.
> I'm ready for this marriage
> to die.
> I want to feel love again.

10/23/00 Loneliness

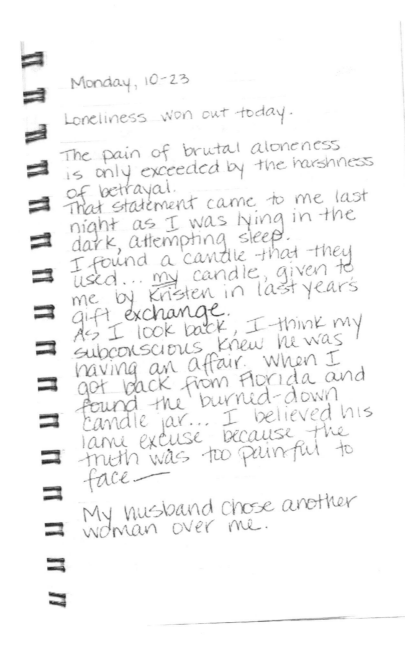

Monday, 10-23

Loneliness won out today.

The pain of brutal aloneness
is only exceeded by the harshness
of betrayal.
That statement came to me last
night as I was lying in the
dark, attempting sleep.
I found a candle that they
used... my candle, given to
me by Kristen in last year's
gift exchange.
As I look back, I think my
subconscious knew he was
having an affair. When I
got back from Florida and
found the burned-down
candle jar... I believed his
lame excuse because the
truth was too painful to
face—

My husband chose another
woman over me.

11/1/00 What Happened?

Wednesday, 11/1

The stupidest things cause me to break down. I was looking at the pictures on Mom & Dad's fridge, and my eyes caught Brent and Kristen's wedding picture ... memories of us both dressed up, very much in love, celebrating with our friends. Then I looked at all the rest of the pictures — all couples, except my lonely school picture with a vast blankness beside. So I lost it, cried my eyes out.

I wanted to love Greg forever. Flaws and all. I wanted to grow old with him, to watch our children grow up around us, not him separate from me.

My school picture — me, alone. In it I'm wearing the blue, flowered dress he got me for our fourth anniversary, the night we stayed at that hotel in downtown Akron. God, what happened to him!?

I wanted to love him forever. When did he quit wanting that too?

11/22/00 One day before Thanksgiving

Wednesday, 11-22

Tomorrow is Thanksgiving.
Where do I start?! God has been
so good to me; in fact, He has
blessed me continually, unceasingly
I heard an explanation of "manna"
today: it was just enough for the
Israelites each day. Just enough
And I got to thinking... I've
had more than enough to get by.
God has given me manna, plus
appetizers and desserts! He has
provided more than my needs.
I cry as I remember all the
people He has used...His people.
What treasures they are. I
have seen FIRSTHAND how the
body of Christ functions. Thank
you, Lord.
And my family. What would I
do without them? They have
been my emotional rocks, my
stability. Without their love,
guidance, support, and empathy
I would be lost, a wreck,
probably still in denial. You
don't choose your family, but
guess what.. I could not have
made a better choice.

12/24/00 My first Christmas Eve alone in six years

Sunday, 12/24

My first Christmas Eve alone in six years. It is so strange. This aloneness is definitely worse than before we were married because at the root of it is betrayal... the knowledge that while I am painfully lonely, Greg has someone to spend his holidays with, someone he apparently cares enough for to leave me and Meghan.

I will be very hurt and angry if he makes no attempt to see Meg tomorrow.

Although I am somewhat depressed, I am also awestruck by the love, support, and generosity of my family... they are the saviors who keep me from drowning in this sea of hurt and pain. God, please bless them above and beyond anything I could imagine. Give them the desires of their hearts. Flood their lives with your presence, allowing them to feel the same closeness I have felt. Thank you, Lord, for loving me through them.

And thank you for the unspeakable, indescribable gift of Your Son.

12/31/00 I remove my wedding rings.

Sunday, 12/31

Well, I just took off my rings.
It wasn't that difficult. The way I
see it, they are the outward
expression of the love that ended
months ago. Still, it caused some
tears. I will miss them for
their aesthetic beauty! They were
gorgeous rings. I remember when
we found the wedding bands.
We both absolutely loved them.
There are so many memories of
our love... good memories. For my
own sake, I'd like to forget most
of them, but I want to remember
some for Meghan's sake. She is
the product of our love; even
though that love has ended, it
doesn't erase the existence of
what once was.
I am anxious for a new year.

God, I trust you to work things
out for my good. Thank you for
blessing me far beyond what I
could ever imagine. Help me to
seek your will for my life, and
bless my precious angel in the
coming year.

Ashes Turned into Beauty

As time went by I had come to terms with the dissolving of my marriage. I had had separation papers drawn up, and in January of 2001, just after the New Year, I had worked up the courage to take off my wedding band. It was painful and scary all at once, but I knew God held me in the palm of His hand, the best place I could be.

The same week, Greg dropped off a letter to me one morning. I was shocked, and I knew it was going to shake me up even more. Reading the letter, I learned he had realized what a mistake he had made, and he wanted to talk. I was so angry! *How could he even entertain the notion of another chance with me?* However, I found myself agreeing to talk with him—and then I agreed to go through counseling with him. Deep inside, all I really wanted was some healing and closure of the gaping wound he had left. But God had other plans.

In the midst of our counseling, I cried out to God that I didn't want Greg, that the hurt was too deep, that the relationship was beyond repair. God's response was silence, but I had a feeling of peace that I could choose either road before me. Certainly, I had grounds for divorce, but I could also choose to reconstruct this damaged marriage. Slowly, over the course of several days, it occurred to me that reconciling was my chance at three very important things:

- rediscovering and reclaiming my first love,
- giving my daughter (and myself) the unbroken family she deserved,

• and having a husband who understood, in very concrete terms, what pornography and infidelity could do to a marriage.

The real question was: *Would I have the courage to take that path?*

1/9/01 Now what do I do?

Tuesday, 1/9

Well, here we are. I knew this day would come. Now what do I do with it? I really had resigned myself to the reality that Greg was not coming back, that our life/lives would be together never again. I have entertained hopes and dreams of a life with someone else, someone focused on God first.

When Greg said he had a letter for me, I knew he was going to ask for a second chance. I just knew. Here I have been praying for God to take my loneliness, for Him to prepare the man he has for me, and quickly! God could have one of two things in store:

#1 — closure — we try this, Greg doesn't have the stamina/strength to go to the end; or #2 — reconciliation — Greg becomes a man of God (1st and foremost), proves himself to me, supports me and Meghan, and we come together.

Either way, a tough road lies ahead. Help me, God. Grant me wisdom and discernment.

❦ Thursday, 2/8

CONFUSION REIGNS.
That's the sum of my feelings.
Everything is weird.
Only God knows my path.
I wish he'd send a map, a clue,
    an itinerary would be great.
Why am I so cynical?!

Lord, I put this mess called
my life in Your complete,
omniscient control. Only You know
what's best, and I trust You
with my whole heart. You are
THE ALMIGHTY God, the One
who never fails, the one who
has sustained me throughout
this crisis.
When I get into my "control-
freak" mode, please remind
me of WHO YOU ARE. You can
do so much more than I, a
mere creation, can.
My sincere prayer is that good
will blossom from this desert.
May ministries spring up because
of it. May I be used of You.
Amen.

2/23/01 Afraid to love again

Saturday Friday, 2/23

I wish I could figure out what I want. I wish the God would enlighten me to this plan. I wish this were easier.
I am feeling more comfortable around him, but... (there's always that but)
I am afraid...
To trust my feelings
To love Greg again
I will crumble & lower my standards
I will let my new closeness with God slip
Of making this decision
Of the effects of it on Meghan

The bottom line is — Can I get over this?

Dear Lord, help me control/deal with my fear in healthy ways. Perfect love casts out all fear, so let your perfect love wash me so I can evaluate this situation without the fog of fear clouding my vision.

3/6/01 Dear Greg,

Letter to Greg, 3/6

Dear Greg,
    I wish I could be as God is
and cast your sin and betrayal
as far as the East is from West.
I wish I could forget all the
pain, anger, and tears that were
direct results of your actions.
It would be so wonderful never
to have to think of these things
again
    But I can't do that. As a human,
it is impossible to erase everything.
However, I do want to move on :
to get to a place where I don't
think of it every day. I'm ready
to heal from these wounds, and
forgiveness is the agent that transforms
these wounds, open and bleeding,
into scars, closed and healed.
Although scars are reminders of
the wound, they certainly don't
hurt as much, and you don't
notice them but occasionally.
    I have taken so long to forgive
you because I wanted it to be
real, perspective-changing forgiveness. I wanted to be ready

I forgive you

to let go of the hurt and betrayal. It sounds silly, but I have clung to it, not because it is enjoyable, but to appease my sense of justice. Until the last few days, when I thought of forgiveness, always after those thoughts came the "buts." but he slept with another woman, but he lied, but he left, and so on. I guess I have finally reached the point where I can, and want to, let go of the "buts." So while I can't be like Jesus in forgetting, I can forgive. In fact, it's my duty, my responsibility as a Christian to forgive. God has shown me so much grace in the sacrifice of His Son for all I have done — and ever will do — wrong, so how can I show another of His creations anything less? The answer is frustrating in its simplicity: I can't.

So, here it is, Greg ... I forgive you. For it all: for lying, for betraying, for leaving, for

I do love you, Cathy

all of it. I have given it all to God, and I truly forgive you.

And now comes "cleanup." I know it's not going to be easy, and I know that odds are against us; but odds don't hold a candle to our God, to His guidance and presence in our lives. He beats any odds. As long as we stay centered in Him, as individuals and as a couple trying to reconcile, I think we can do this.

I have seen real change in you, Greg, and I hope you are motivated to continue in that line of change, and to never ever return, even for an instant, to those old habits.

So now we need to strive for this ...

Christian married love is the persistent effort on the part of two people to create for each other the circumstances in which each can become the person God intended him/her to be: a better person than he/she could become alone.

I do love you, Cathy

Pulled, stretched, yanked around
Like a rag doll
Whose arms are fraying and tattered
Keeping it all together
Can be so hard, so stressing

Giving up is not an option
Yet I feel it
Tugging at my heart
From my mind
Which wonders why I'm still here

Well, God had given me the courage I needed to reconcile with my husband. Greg and I have become living proof that God still works miracles.

It took six months of very intense counseling and a complete turnaround for Greg, but with God's help, we put back together our shattered remains of a marriage. On July 15, 2001, in front of our closest friends and family, we renewed our vows.

People always talk of the miracle God did in Greg's life, but I think that the more miraculous act was the "heart surgery" God performed on me. The bitterness and anger I overcame was nothing short of divine intervention, as God Himself reached down and healed my broken heart with His grace-filled hand.

FOR THE SECOND TIME

July 15, 2001

Complete amazement filled my heart as I sat in the church with my husband, my closest friends, and my dear family. Even though I had been the chief planner of this event, I was still awestruck that it was actually happening. As my pastor spoke about God's grace and second chances to all of us gathered there, I tried to focus on his words, wanting to remember the details. But my mind drifted . . .

I contemplated God's sense of humor and irony. *Was it just seven months ago that I finally resigned myself to the fact that my marriage was over, finally made the decision to remove my wedding band?* I had long since put the engagement ring away, tucked deep in a drawer I rarely used. That ring was too pretty for our situation, too beautiful for the ugliness that took root in my heart when he had left. But I had clung to the wedding band for six months, hoping against all odds that our marriage could somehow survive the devastating blow of betrayal. Those early days were so difficult. Greg's affair and abandonment of our marriage had crumbled me: for a solid month I cried on a daily basis. Eventually, though, I faced reality. More importantly, I learned to put my complete faith and trust in God, knowing that He was holding the shattered pieces of my heart—and that was the best place my heart could ever be.

I remembered my reaction to Greg's note, his plea for our marriage delivered six months after he had left. *How dare he ask for another chance! How dare he even entertain the notion of forgiveness! Who does he think he is?* I distinctly recall having looked skyward to say, "No! This is *not* happening!" and wondering what God had up His sleeve.

Eventually, I had calmed down. Greg and I had talked extensively, we had cried, I had laid out some ground rules, and we had decided to seek counseling.

We were still separated, he at his apartment and I at our house. I didn't say it to him then, but in my heart, I wanted the counseling for the sole purpose of healing and finding closure in *ending* this mess of a marriage. I still had a gaping emotional wound, and counseling seemed the only way to stitch it up. Nothing in my plans included reconciling with Greg. No. Not after six months of him living the life of a rebellious teen-cheating spouse. I had recently found and was able to cling to some peace and a glimmer of hope for the future. *Now here he is, trying to cloud my skies again.*

Did I mention God's sense of humor and irony? About a month into our counseling, an irritating revelation hit me: *I still love this jerk.* How could I? I hated the things he had done with a deep passion Then came more of God's irony. I came to a Bible story I had never read before: the story of Hosea and Gomer in the Book of Hosea.

God told Hosea to take back his unfaithful wife so the people of Israel would see his example as an analogy: God would always take back the wayward Israelites, no matter what horrible sins they committed, if they truly repented and returned to Him.

I slammed my Bible down on the bed and commenced with part two of my heavenward glance and rejection of the idea. "No way!" was part of my speech to the Almighty. Committing right then that I was not going to become a Hosea, God saw an angry piece of my mind.

His answer seemed to be silence. But over the following weeks, I felt a sense of His grace and acceptance. It was as though He was trying to tell me that I had every right as well as biblical backup for divorce, but I could also try to make it work.

A few months later, another realization hit me. Because of our intense counseling sessions, Greg knew, in very clear terms, the boundaries of a marriage. He understood all too well what his betrayal had done to me, and he was now concretely aware of the dangers of infidelity and other breaches of trust. If I could only overcome my hurt, there was the chance to have a spouse who completely understood our boundaries, knew everything about me, and with whom I had a long and happy past, excluding the recent months. In addition, I couldn't forget that he was the father of my child.

While those thoughts were exhilarating, they were also terrifying. They made me want to wrap myself in a blanket and hide. Could I actually make myself so vulnerable to a person who had cut me with the knife of betrayal so deep that I still had scars? The thought staggered me.

Yet, as time passed, here we were, in the same church in which we were married seven years prior. It certainly wasn't easy, making myself that vulnerable—but I wasn't alone. In those months, I came to know God on a level I had never experienced, and it was through His strength that I was able to walk down the long corridor of forgiveness and reconciliation. His example was the beacon I followed in those difficult days: *if He in the midst of betrayal and deceit could die on the Cross for all of humanity—if He could be the perfect picture of forgiveness—then who am I to withhold forgiveness from someone He has deemed worthy?*

Vows! The pastor was calling us up to recite them. Greg and I grabbed our papers and walked up front, faced each other and held hands. I glanced at our family and friends, so grateful for their support and love, and I smiled at our little girl in the lap of her grandmother. Sure, this road was going to be bumpy and fraught with challenges, but I had a bold, crazy confidence. I knew our roots ran deep, and I trusted in our God, Who has our best interests at heart. Furthermore, I had seen real and extreme change in Greg. That was key.

Most of all, I had peace. Finally! A peace that was inexplicable, that went beyond what mere words could describe. It is a supernatural peace that somehow had grown from the rubble, from the pain . . . out of nowhere.

PROVIDENTIAL SERENDIPITY

October 2012

Awe-inspiring
To see my pain and heartache move from
An all-consuming blaze to
A steady burn and then
A smoldering pile
That is now morphing into
A sterilizing ember.

I am simply amazed.
God promises He will turn our ashes into beauty
But to LIVE that, to WITNESS first-hand
The fully receded waters after the earth-changing flood . . .

I am redeemed
In so many ways

Rainbow Verses **3**

When it looked like the sun wasn't going to shine anymore,
God put a rainbow in the clouds.

—Maya Angelou

From my journal or index cards, notes on cards from sweet people, or
directly from the Bible, I collected an arsenal of verses, each one encouraging and uplifting when I needed it the most.

After Greg and I reconciled, and I looked over these verses, I realized
what a treasure they are. Without my noticing, God had "put a rainbow
in the clouds," one "color" at a time, given according to my need. I felt the
power of God intervene in my life through these Scriptures, using them to
help me overcome in the battle for my life, my marriage, my family.

> *The righteous cry out, and the Lord hears them; he delivers them*
> *from all their troubles. The Lord is close to the brokenhearted*
> *and saves those who are crushed in spirit.*
>
> —Psalm 34:17–18 (NIV)

I wrote this verse in my journal about five weeks after Greg left me, but
I had committed it to memory weeks before that. Although I can't recall
the exact date, this verse jumped off the page one night when I was feeling
particularly "brokenhearted." It empowered me with such hope that I still
feel moved and blessed by it whenever I read it. I remember, yes, this verse
is truth. I know because I lived it. God was definitely close to my broken
heart and He saved my crushed spirit.

Peace I leave with you; my peace I give you. I do not give to you as the world gives. Do not let your hearts be troubled and do not be afraid.

—John 14:27 (NIV)

I was so scared in the first few weeks after Greg left. The aloneness of my heart, the quietness of my house (even with a newborn), and the despair in my mind all combined to pack quite a fearful assault. I rejoiced in this verse because it assured me that God's peace is otherworldly, supernatural, and transcendent. It is not meant to be understood but simply received. Reading this verse over and over gave me a peace that fought back and drove the fear away.

Give all your worries to him, because he cares for you. Control yourselves and be careful! The devil, your enemy, goes around like a roaring lion looking or someone to eat. Refuse to give in to him, by standing strong in your faith. . . . And after you suffer for a short time, God, who gives all grace, will make everything right. he will make you strong and support you and keep you from falling.

—1 Peter 5:7–10 (NCV)

These verses were written in my journal right below the title, "When I needed encouragement" and had no commentary from me. As I think back, this was all I needed—no commentary necessary. It assured me that God *sees* me, He *knows* me, He *loves* me, and He will make everything *right*. Near this page in my journal were the lyrics to a song by Kathy Troccoli: "He Will Make a Way"— "He can deliver in the darkest of days / There is no war He doesn't win / When you're at your end / He's just beginning."

Why, my soul, are you downcast? Why so disturbed within me? Put your hope in God, for I will yet praise him, my Savior and my God. —Psalm 42:11 (NIV)

What stood out to me about this verse is that David repeated it three times within two chapters. Since he was a songwriter, I'm sure it was a refrain, a chorus. I couldn't help but wonder if his life also was getting to be . . . too much. I recorded this verse and adopted David's mentality. When we don't feel like praising, we should do so anyway, and our attitude will follow. Make a mental shift from self to Savior.

> *But you, God, see the trouble of the afflicted; you consider their*
> *grief and take it in hand.*
>
> —Psalm 10:14 (NIV)

God sees me. I could really just stop right there. I have a Creator and He sees me, right where I am, in the middle of the muck and grime. Not only that, but God takes my grief in hand! He sees me and He works for my good, works to pull me out of the muck and grime. This verse still brings tears to my eyes. We have a Savior who cares for us. Especially when Greg's leaving was fresh and the pain so raw, I needed to hear this.

> *He reached down from on high and took hold of me; he drew*
> *me out of deep waters.*
>
> —Psalm 18:16 (NIV)

Wow, I sure knew what deep waters were. Sometimes I felt as if I were treading water, just barely keeping my head above the waves, and then life would throw me a ten-pound brick. But every time that happened, every time life threw a brick, God *moved*, either through His Word, His Spirit, or His people. I remember several times when I would get a bill with no means to pay it; I would feel fear and worry had a knot in my stomach. But God was faithful. Every time He intervened, often through an unexpected gift from a friend, co-worker, family member, or even an acquaintance. They always said the same type of thing: "God told me to give this to you" or "God impressed me to pray [something specific] for you." On several occasions, what was given to me was eerily close to what I needed. It was amazing to be in deep waters and just watch God *work*. I was blessed, even in deep waters, I was *blessed*.

> *I remain confident of this: I will see the goodness of the Lord in the land of the living. Wait for the Lord; be strong and take heart and wait for the Lord.*
> —Psalm 27:13–14 (NIV)

This passage reduced me to tears in seconds. I was having one of those days where I just couldn't see any light at the end of the tunnel. I had already been praying to God those prayers of desperation where I asked Him to make it all go away. I was unsure of everything, and after a long day, I opened my Bible to Psalm 27, my eyes falling on this passage. It was as if God, once again, was whispering in my ear, holding me close. He reminded me of His care for me over the last few months and how He provided more than I needed. This passage pivoted my perspective, and I could trust again. We can remember, He is the Almighty, the Creator of the universe. He's got this.

> *Forget the former things; do not dwell on the past. See, I am doing a new thing! Now it springs up; do you not perceive it? I am making a way in the desert and streams in the wasteland.*
> —Isaiah 43:18–19 (NIV)

I have an entire page in my journal devoted to this passage. I had just met with my lawyer and moved forward with filing separation papers. I remember she introduced me to the term dissolutionment—and it was so harsh. However, Greg had been gone for two months with absolutely no intention to return, and I had been praying for weeks that God would nudge me away from this decision of legal separation if it were not His will. After hearing the story, my lawyer was surprised I had waited two months. So that evening, after putting Meghan to bed, I was still wrestling with thought, did I do the right thing? I knelt by my bed and opened my Bible to the Book of Isaiah because a friend had told me about a verse there. I was reading subject headings when the above verses stood out—as though illuminated with neon arrows.

> *Hear my cry, O God; listen to my prayer. From the ends of the earth I call to you, I call as my heart grows faint; lead me to the rock that is higher than I. For you have been my refuge, a strong tower against the foe.*
>
> —Psalm 61:1–3 (NIV)

As time passed in the midst of my trial, the situation became easier to handle, partly because it wasn't a fresh, open wound anymore and partly because God was strengthening me. However, I still had breakdowns. One day, I felt particularly *small* and *hidden*, like God wasn't seeing me. I found this passage, immediately highlighted it in my Bible, and prayed it aloud. Instantly, I felt His presence, and in my next sentence, I was apologizing once again for my doubt. Doesn't it help to know that David, the man after God's own heart, felt this way too?

> *God is our refuge and strength, an ever-present help in trouble. Therefore we will not fear, though the earth give way and the mountains fall into the heart of the sea, though its waters roar and foam and the mountains quake with their surging.*
>
> —Psalm 46:1–3 (NIV)

Finally, a picture that seemed more hectic than my life! If God could be "an ever-present help" in this kind of trouble, then surely my mere marital strife would be covered too. I found such hope in this passage and claimed it as my own, believing that God would always be my refuge and strength. He would be more than enough.

Lord my God, I called to you for help, and you healed me. You, Lord, brought me up from the realm of the dead; you spared me from going down to the pit.

—Psalm 30:2–3 (NIV)

I remember when I first had the courage to take off my wedding band. I had quit wearing the engagement ring long before, but it was so hard to remove that wedding band. I didn't want to admit failure, defeat, divorce, but as the new year approached, I began to see things differently. God had healed me; He was still healing me. It would be a long process, but I knew I wasn't "going down to the pit." God would work everything out for my good. Of that I was certain, and a band on my finger didn't change His promises.

Though you have made me see troubles, many and bitter, you will restore my life again; from the depths of the earth you will again bring me up. You will increase my honor and comfort me once more.

—Psalm 71:20–21 (NIV)

Count the *again*s in that passage . . . three. On the page where I wrote this passage in my journal are also lyrics from a song titled "Job" by Cindy Morgan. I had reflected on how Job was able (shockingly) to keep his faith and trust in God, even when he felt abandoned. *No matter what*—and those words are *key*—Job believed in his future; he knew in shose hands it rested. I could identify with that! Job was such an encouragement to me. If an Old Testament follower of God, who didn't have the example of Christ could *trust so blindly*, then so could I. Right then I decided that I would fully give the reins of my life to God. The day I recorded this verse in my journal was five days before Greg informed me that he wanted a second chance.

Part 2
Winning in the War

 Greg Dyer says he wished this resource had been available when he and Cathy needed it to help overcome his addiction to pornography.

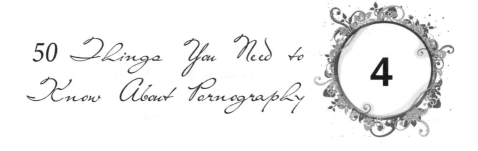

50 Things You Need to Know About Pornography

4

> **"Pornography is the defining sexual sin of our day."**
> —Heath Lambert

Someone you know, someone you love, is struggling with pornography. Pornography, if it has not already, will affect to some degree every Christian home. Sadly, many have chosen either to ignore the issue or deny that it is a problem in the church. That simply must end now. Pornography is the new bubonic plague.

I am not suggesting that your husband is looking at pornography or that your son or daughter is. However, most men in the church are dealing with some level of struggle.

The issue is awkward, sensitive, and even embarrassing to broach, but I believe that Christian women are the key to helping this issue come to the forefront of discussion. Through prayer and discussion, the women of God can encourage their husbands, sons—as well as their pastors—to bring the issue out of the darkness and into the light.

The statistics are overwhelming. Some researchers attest that half of pastors are battling with this issue personally. Satan has found a way to effectively silence Christian men in their leadership roles in the home and church. This shame-based sin makes Christian men feel alone in their struggle and that they simply cannot divulge their struggle. That is one of the main reasons to challenge 1 million Christian men in all churches and denominations to commit to living a pornography-free life.

This book encourages discussions about pornography in the church. This opens the door for discussion in churches and gives Christian women an opportunity to address the subject with their husbands, sons, fiancés, and pastors.

Every day, more Christian women discover their husbands are looking at pornography. The effects can be devastating. Each week, more Christian women discover their sons have been viewing pornography on the Internet. Another Christian woman hears of a marriage breaking up because of porn or of another pastor or Christian leader who has fallen because he chose with a click of the mouse to enter a pornographic Web site and then kept going back.

Men you would least suspect are finding themselves in the most enslaving habit perhaps ever. There are many reasons why pornography is as addictive or more addictive than crack cocaine. As a pastor, I continually deal with the devastation a husband's pornography habit has wreaked on the marriage and home.

So what can you do? Plenty. We can win this battle, but not without a fight on your part.

Although more women are increasingly struggling personally with viewing pornography, this is still an issue affecting the majority of men, Christian men. Listen to this statistical summary from Baylor University's Counseling Center's Web site:

> Four in every five Christians believe pornography to be morally unacceptable, yet these stories are not so far from those told by many Christians. For a time Christians may escape the allure of pornography, but all too often the problem is as significant for Christians as non-Christians. In fact, 47% of Christians admitted pornography was a major problem in their home in a survey conducted by Internet Filter Review. Even more discouraging are the 53% of men belonging to the Christian group Promise Keepers who admit to visiting pornography

sites every week. Christians may claim a different standard,
but they still struggle with the same pornographic issues.

Unfortunately, the situation is not much better among Christian pastors. A survey of evangelical Protestant clergy conducted by The Leadership Survey in 2001 found that 40 percent of those responding struggled with pornography. Another survey in 2002 conducted by Rick Warren of Saddleback Church found that in the previous month, 30 percent of pastors had viewed pornography.

Apparently pornography does not show bias toward one's religious affiliation or lack thereof. Some positive statistical differences exist between Christians and non-Christians. For example, Christians have a slightly later age of first exposure to pornography. However, Christians still seem to have all the same issues with pornography non-Christians experience.

Our Opportunity

Women in every church have a window of opportunity to make a difference in this matter. However, that window is quickly closing. You must seize the moment and passionately feel the call to action. As a Christian woman you must become armed with information, impassioned through prayer, and biased toward specific action. Christian women must stand and say, "Not in my marriage, not in my home, and not in my church!"

Let me clearly say that this message is for Christians. Outside of Christ, there is no hope I can offer. This is written specifically for Christians and from a clear biblical perspective. Although I am not judging those who are outside of Christ for their pornography struggles (they need Christ before they can hope to have overcoming power), I am judging Christians who look at pornography. The Bible is clear about the issue of lust.

A popular trilogy has sold more than 65 million copies. Even Christian women are reading these books which have been called erotic fiction, mommy porn, or soft porn. This is the fastest selling paperback of all time surpassing even *Harry Potter.* Erotic scenes featuring perverted sexual activities are the themes of the book.

The interest among professing Christian women was such that I felt I needed to address it in a sermon called, "50 Reasons Why Christians Shouldn't Read *Fifty Shades of Grey*." Preaching 50 points was a great challenge in a 25-minute period. In this chapter, we will take the idea and format used in that message and share 50 things every Christian woman needs to know about pornography.

1. Men are wired to be stimulated visually, making pornography appealing.

No man, including a Christian man, is immune from being affected by what he sees. When Adam saw Eve, he was affected by what he saw. The breakdown of men and women who view pornography is 72 percent male, 28 percent female. God hardwired men to be stimulated visually. That is true for your husband, son, fiancé, or any man. What a man sees affects *what* he thinks about and *how* he thinks. That's reflected in what Job shared in this statement: "I made a covenant with my eyes not to look lustfully at a young woman" (Job 31:1 NIV).

Pornography is the enemy's perfect tool to tempt men. In the book *The Drug of the New Millennium: The Brain Science Behind Internet Pornography Use*, Mark B. Kastleman writes, "The male brain is structured in a way that makes it more susceptible to pornographic images. It makes little difference whether a porn viewer is a 12-year-old boy or a 70-year-old man." One look at pornography has the power to hook a man for life. It is that powerful.

2. Satan bombards a man's eyes daily through media.

Our enemy understands how to utilize media to affect the eyes of men for the purpose of eliciting a response. Whether it is through television, billboards, magazines, advertisements, Internet, or mobile phone, Christian men are being bombarded with sexual images everywhere they go, every day. Those images become thoughts and thoughts can become fantasies and fantasies become sexual sin, unless those thoughts are interrupted with God's truth. No wonder Proverbs 4:23 says, "Above all else, guard your heart, for everything you do flows from it" (NIV).

3. The primary means of pornographic temptation is the Internet.

The Internet is the number one tool Satan uses to tempt men to look at pornography. The Internet has made pornography readily available—where once a man would have to buy a magazine, buy or rent a video, or go to some seedy, dark, sex shop to view pornography. Now porn is available any time of the day or night. At this writing, there are more than 500 million pornographic pages online.

The Internet has also made pornography affordable. In fact, much of pornography is free. It provides anonymity, or at least the lie that makes a man think *no one will ever have to know*. Men who would not go to a sex shop will go to a pornographic Web site. The Internet has been called the "crack cocaine of pornography." You can see why Internet filtering and blocking software are essential for every computer in your possession.

According to a survey published in the *Journal of the American Psychological Association*, 86 percent of men are likely to click on Internet sex sites if given the opportunity.

4. The average age of first Internet pornography exposure is between 10 and 11 years old.

Much of this exposure takes place by accident while a child is working on homework, playing a game, or surfing the Internet. Ninety percent of 8- to 16-year-olds have viewed porn online mostly while doing homework, according to freedomyou.com.

Family Safe Media reports that the largest group of viewers of Internet pornography is boys between ages 12 and 17. Christian Broadcast News recently reported, "Today's young generation receives more temptations per second than any other generation in the history of mankind."

Alarmingly, the age at which children begin looking at porn will continue to decrease. Once viewed, that image is forever imbedded in the mind of a child. No child is immune and no home, even a Christian home, can make assumptions such as, "It won't happen to my child."

Specific preventive steps are essential in protecting your child, steps such as installing filtering and accountability software, close monitoring of the home computer and monitoring the child's choice of friends. To be effective this must be done by loving, warm, boundary-setting, and communicative parents. Remarkably, many reliable sources have reported alarming statistics: a small percentage of parents have set rules for what their kids can do on the computer.

5. The word *pornography* means "writing about prostitutes."

As I was leading a conference, a seasoned pastor asked me, "What does the word *pornography* mean? No one has ever told me."

Pornography comes from a Greek word that means "writings about prostitutes." In other words, writing about the activities of prostitutes in such a way that this brings sexual arousal. Now, that definition is expanded to include any sexual images or activities that stimulate sexual arousal. *Webster's* defines *pornography* as "the depiction of erotic behavior (as in pictures or writing) intended to cause sexual excitement."

The purpose of pornography is to bring sexual excitement divorced from intimate relationship. The pornography industry only focuses on the physical aspect, leaving the spiritual and emotional aspects dissociated—leading to emptiness.

6. Most Christian men are struggling with pornography.

A recent Life Christian Resource poll of 1,000 pastors indicated that 62 percent of them believe 10 percent or less of the men in their churches are struggling with pornography. My thought would be: that number is realistically at least 80 percent. I am not suggesting that 80 percent of the men in churches are addicted to pornography. I am suggesting, however, that they are struggling at some level with looking at pornography.

There is porn in the pew—not literally—but sitting in every church, every Sunday, the majority of men are struggling. The problem has been that broaching the subject is awkward, embarrassing, and sensitive. While we deny the fact of Christian men viewing pornography, men are filled with shame and guilt, feeling all alone, and trapped with seemingly no way out.

7. **Some Christian men are more tempted than others to look at pornography.**
Much depends upon a man's past experiences and events and his present spiritual, emotional, and physical condition. If a Christian man is dealing with abuse or abandonment issues of the past, this can greatly contribute to the temptation to look at pornography (although nothing excuses it). Exposure to pornography at a young age further contributes to the temptation.

Wendy and Larry Maltz, in their book *The Porn Trap: The Essential Guide to Overcoming Problems Caused by Pornography,* suggest: "If you have issues with porn today, chances are they can be traced back to your early encounters with pornography."

When a Christian man allows a sinful thought to stay in his mind, is not practicing spiritual disciplines, has unmet emotional needs, is in a season of unusual emotional or physical stress, has lack of intimacy in his marriage, or has a painful past, these contribute to the temptation to medicate the pain through the click of a mouse.

8. **Pornography demeans and degrades women.**
Pornography harms women physically, emotionally, relationally, and mentally. Today's porn creates an image that sex is only for a man's pleasure and includes any activity that a man desires. A 2011 study in the Archives of Sexual Behavior found that 36 percent of women surveyed consider porn use as being unfaithful. More than 40 percent of women feel their partner's porn use means that she's "not good enough," according to Elizabeth Lawson, in "Smut Check," published in *Men's Health.*

In another study, "The Social Costs of Pornography," the authors state:

> Today's consumption of Internet pornography can harm women in particular. Indeed any woman can be affected, insofar as pornography shapes cultural expectations about female sexual behavior. In North American and Western European culture, wives generally seek marital relationships founded upon mutual respect, honesty, shared power, and romantic

love. Pornography as depicted on the Internet enshrines the opposite: relationships based on disrespect, detachment, promiscuity, and often abuse.

The Porn Harms Web site gives us a window into the pornography industry's attitude toward women:

> The actual making of pornography often involves violence and sexual assault. During the production of commercial pornography, performers are subjected to intense abuse and violence and are pressured to continue by their agent or director.

A Christian man who views pornography begins to use his wife as a sexual outlet, rather than as a partner in a meaningful moment of intimacy.

9. Pornography causes men to "objectify" women.

Porn causes men to look at women differently. A Christian man who views pornography looks at women through a lust-filled lens. Pornography has the effect of objectifying women as sexual objects. Paul tells us to treat "older women as mothers, and the younger women as sisters, in all purity" (1 Timothy 5:2 ESV).

In a 2008 article from *Psychology Today* the writer reported: "Pornography itself is about the objectification of women. In this context, women are treated as things, receptacles and socially dissociated objects to be used and tossed aside."

Objectification defined: "An attitude in which women are objects rated by size, shape and harmony of body parts; sexual fantasy leads to emotional unavailability and dissatisfaction" (CovenantEyes.com/porn). In one widely reported study, according to the Witherspoon Institute publication, *The Social Costs of Pornography,* in February 2009, Susan Fiske, professor of psychology at Princeton University, used MRI (magnetic resonance imaging) scans to analyze the brain activity of men viewing pornography. The results showed that, after viewing pornographic images, men looked at women more as objects than as humans."

10. Pornography only focuses on the physical, disconnecting the spiritual and emotional elements of sex.

I believe that God made humans three-dimensional—body, soul, and spirit. In Christian marriage, each of these aspects is vitally important to the relationship with the spiritual part (our relationship with God) directing the body and soul. However, in pornography, only the physical aspect is the focus.

Even in marriage, a Christian man who is hooked on pornography primarily desires to bring pleasure to himself. Sex becomes a physical act only, something God never intended. Sex is something to be given to your mate, not demanded. "Now Adam knew Eve his wife" (Genesis 4:1 ESV). The Hebrew word for *knew* incorporates all three elements—body, soul, and spirit. To disconnect these means emptiness, pain, and hurt.

11. Pornography is addictive.

Again, the nature of pornography, especially Internet pornography, is addictive to a man's brain. Numerous studies have proven this fact. Porn, like crack cocaine, alcohol, and gambling, is habit-forming. Continued pornography use affects the part of the brain that forms addictions.

On the Web site fightthenewdrug.org, the question "How is porn addictive" is answered showing how pornography affects a man's brain. Three words are used to explain: *Chemicals, Rewiring,* and *Dependency.*

First, a man overexposes his brain with pleasure chemicals like dopamine, serotonin, oxytocin, and epinephrine through habitually viewing pornography. Secondly, a man's brain rewires itself to accommodate the extra chemicals. Thirdly, he builds up a tolerance and a dependency to the chemicals. He goes from wanting the pleasure chemicals, in order to feel good, to needing them. The area of the brain responsible for making decisions and logically thinking through situations and scenarios (frontal lobes) is the part of the brain most affected by addiction.

12. Pornography is accessible anytime.

No wife could be available to have sex with her husband all hours of the day or night. That is impossible. However, Internet pornography promises to always be there, no matter where, no matter what, no matter when. That makes the temptation greater and more serious. Pornography's online shops never close, never shut down for vacation, or take a break. Interestingly enough, the day of the week that pornography sites are most searched is Sunday. It is always there; never says no or not now or "I don't feel like it," and promises to bring happiness and excitement. Of course, it is Satan's trap, but the availability is a big part of the appeal.

13. Pornography silences Christian men.

As a pastor, I have seen firsthand how pornography silences a Christian man from being the spiritual leader in his home and church. His witness, his praise, his encouragement to others, his helping others to grow spiritually—it's all duct-taped (spiritually speaking). David cried out to God after his sin with Bathsheba, "O Lord, open my lips, That my mouth may declare Your praise" (Psalm 51:15). Sin silences a Christian's praise to God. Pornography removes a Christian man's sense of moral authority.

14. Pornography creates amnesia in the man who views it.

When a man is viewing pornography he forgets everything that is important to him—God, his wife, his fiancée, his children, his witness for Christ, and the consequences. Everyone and everything around him is blocked out and his focus is only on the moment of looking at pornography. Kastleman, in *The Drug of the New Millennium,* explains this as the "Funnel of Sexual Arousal and the Narrowing Process."

For hours, a man can be consumed while looking at pornography because all sense of time and responsibility is lost. When a man is looking at pornography, he can think of nothing else. However, once a man acts out, usually through masturbation, he begins to feel the shame, guilt, and sense of *I cannot believe what I just did.* Usually that follows with a promise that he will never look at pornography again. But, the lure of pornography keeps pulling him back.

15. Pornography viewing is adultery.

Jesus said, "But I say, anyone who even looks at a woman with lust has already committed adultery with her in his heart" (Matthew 5:28 NLT). Internet pornography (or any porn) invites men to be unfaithful to their wives. A man is lusting after someone other than his wife.

Although the initial consequences of viewing pornography and having a physical affair are different, it is still adultery. No Christian woman would believe that pornography viewing by her husband is not betrayal and adultery. Pornography is "an insult, it is disloyal, and it is cheating," writes Dr. Phil McGraw.

16. Most Christian men feel alone in their struggle with pornography.

This is what Satan is using to bring shame to men. Most Christian men who struggle with pornography believe that they are pretty much alone in that struggle. Honestly, if a Christian man asked another Christian man if this is a problem for him, he would probably get no for an answer. Thus he continues to suffer in silence and shame.

What I have discovered through the programs in the church that I pastor is that once men understand that they are not struggling alone, God has an opportunity to bring repentance, healing, and accountability. That is why it is essential to broach the subject in church.

17. Men struggling with pornography have triggers.

A trigger is that which places a man in an atmosphere encouraging him to act out sexually. Triggers can be different for each man. There are times, places, situations, and people that cause each person to be more vulnerable to sexual sin. One Christian man confessed that as he lay in his bed at night and his wife went to sleep, he could see the glow of the computer screen and that became a trigger for him to start thinking about looking at pornography.

18. There are rituals a man goes through before viewing pornography.

A man who views pornography goes through rituals or routines in order to get to the point of actually viewing it. A ritual is what a man does (the steps he takes) to get ready to look at pornography. When a man starts thinking about looking at pornography, the rituals normally begin.

The battle is lost or won before a man begins the rituals. If the thought of looking at pornography is not dealt with—that imagination taken captive to God's will—the next step will be going through the process of getting to the point of viewing pornography and acting out sexually, usually through masturbation. Mark Laaser, Faithful and True Ministries, writes, "When the ritual begins the battle is lost."

A trigger affects the thoughts and the thoughts, if not interrupted and placed in captivity to God's will, through the power of Christ, will lead to the process of looking at pornography.

The Christian man must build exits before the rituals begin. That's what Paul teaches in 1 Corinthians 10:13:

> No temptation has overtaken you but such as is common to man; and God is faithful, who will not allow you to be tempted beyond what you are able, but with the temptation will provide the way of escape also, so that you will be able to endure it.

Rehearsing the exit strategy before the temptation is essential.

19. Pornography knows no age boundaries.

At a conference I was leading in Albany, New York, an 81-year-old man approached me and said, "I was 80 when I broke free from sexual bondage." Pornography affects all ages from 5 to 100. The largest consumer of Internet pornography by age group is 35 to 49. 90 percent of 8- to 16-year-olds have viewed porn online, mostly while doing homework. Among children the largest consumer of Internet porn is aged 12 to 17.

With the increase in pornography consumption, older adult males are driving the sales of erectile dysfunction drugs. That is not to suggest that everyone who takes one of these medications is hooked on pornography. Rather, it is having an effect on men's ability to respond sexually to their wives due to the stimulation that some now experience only as a result of viewing pornography.

20. Pornography kills whatever it touches.

Pornography has the touch of death. The stress of a Christian man living a double life kills his intimacy with God and his wife. Pornography kills marriages, kills a dad's relationship with his children, kills creativity, kills intimacy with God and his wife, kills his witness, kills his praise to God, kills love, kills time, kills respect, kills the innocence of children who see it, kills the blessings of God, and can kill his future. James reminds us:

> Don't let anyone under pressure to give in to evil say, "God is trying to trip me up." God is impervious to evil, and puts evil in no one's way. The temptation to give in to evil comes from us and only us. We have no one to blame but the leering, seducing flare-up of our own lust. Lust gets pregnant, and has a baby: sin! Sin grows up to adulthood, and becomes a real killer" (James 1:13–15 The Message).

21. Pornography's appeal is anonymity.

This sin is nearly always couched in secrecy. Seventy percent of those who view pornography keep their habit a secret according to author Michael Leahy, *Porn @ Work*.

Pornography's promise of anonymity and secrecy become tools of temptation. Can't you hear Satan saying, *No one will ever know and you are not hurting anyone else. Besides, with all the stress you are under, you deserve some pleasure.* There is enslaving power in a secret. When God's light is allowed to shine on that secret, freedom can begin.

22. Pornography defiles rather than enhances marriage.

The world outside of Christ often counsels couples to watch porn together to spice up their sex life or love life. No Christian couple should ever, under any circumstances, allow pornography into their home or watch pornography in an attempt to bring excitement to their marriage. Yes, every couple should work on making their marriage, including their sex life, more exciting, but never by using pornography. That would be like inviting a thief into your home to teach you the value of your possessions.

"Marriage is be held in honor among all, and the marriage bed is to be undefiled; for fornicators and adulterers God will judge" (Hebrews 13:4).

Defile has the idea of soiling or impurity. A husband viewing pornography is one way the Christian marriage bed is defiled. An example of an equally destructive activity is for a Christian wife to read the "Fifty Shades" trilogy in hopes of spicing up her love life. This places her stamp of approval on pornography and gives it some kind of value.

23. Pornography decreases sexual satisfaction within marriage.

No wife can live up to what is portrayed in pornography. The false images attempt to convince a man that he must look outside his marriage to find sexual fulfillment. The media increasingly presents sex within marriage as boring and sex outside of marriage as exciting and to be desired. A man will compare what he has seen in pornography with his wife's appearance and their sex life. Pornography robs couples of the joy, excitement, and fulfillment of God's great gift of sex in marriage. No Christian marriage is made better, more successful, more intimate, or happier by the husband viewing pornography.

Professors Dolf Zillman of Indiana University and Jennings Bryant of the University of Houston have found that repeated exposure to pornography results in a decreased satisfaction with one's sexual partner (marriagemissions.com).

No woman can compete with what is seen in pornography. The activities portrayed in pornography are not consistent with real life, yet a man can easily begin to think that if he is not experiencing what he sees in those scenes, then he is missing out, thus making him wonder why his wife isn't like the porn star.

"Drink waters out of your own cistern [of a pure marriage relationship], and fresh running waters out of your own well" (Proverbs 5:15 AMP).

24. Pornography can become an idol.

Many Christian men who are struggling with pornography spend hours thinking about it, planning when/where/how to watch it, spending focused time and attention away from God and family on what has become the dominating force of their life. Pornography idolizes an image, the image of a female body. It demands first place in a man's thoughts, time, energy, and emotions. An idol is anything you put ahead of God or instead of God. God demands first place. Pornography demands first place. You choose (Exodus 20:3–5).

25. Pornography has an escalating effect.

A man who views pornography, and continues viewing it, will not stay at that level. It will escalate in its path of destruction. The nature of porn is to create a desire for more and more and more. The same pornographic image that stimulated a man when he began viewing porn will soon not be enough; it will take more to bring the same excitement. "The turning point for most men is when they get caught either by their wives, their bosses, or by the police," writes Meg Wilson, in *Hope After Betrayal: Healing When Sexual Addiction Invades Your Marriage*.

Pornharmsresearch.com reported in 2011:

> Consumers graduate from common to less common forms of pornography as their usage increases over time. This may be because familiar material becomes unexciting as a result of habituation. These consumers move to more violent and degrading materials as they become invested more in pornography.

Dr. Victor B. Cline, at covenanteyes.com, writes in "Pornography's Effects on Adults and Children," about the "four-factor syndrome" common to all his sex addiction clients:

ADDICTION: Pornography provides a powerful sexual stimulant or aphrodisiac effect, followed by sexual release, most often through masturbation.

ESCALATION: Over time addicts require more explicit and deviant material to meet their sexual "needs."

DESENSITIZATION: What was first perceived as gross, shocking and disturbing, in time becomes common and acceptable.

ACTING OUT SEXUALLY: This fourth phase is an increasing tendency to act out sexually the behaviors viewed in the pornography that the porn-consumer had been repeatedly exposed to.

26. Pornography has two different distinctions.

Those distinctions are softcore and hardcore.

Softcore pornography is less explicit than hardcore material in depicting or describing sexual activity.

Hardcore pornography is an extreme form of pornography that features explicit sexual acts. The term was coined in the second half of the twentieth century to distinguish it from softcore pornography. It usually takes the form of photographs, often displayed in magazines or on the Internet or in films. It can even appear as a cartoon. Since the 1990s it has been distributed widely over the Internet.)

For the Christian, both softcore and hardcore pornography are off-limits since both are designed to create a desire that cannot be fulfilled within the will of God.

27. Pornography never has a neutral effect.

Pornography always has an effect. A Christian man's mind, emotions, and spirit are never the same after viewing pornography. It alters his opinions, refocuses his eyes, messes with his emotions, distances him from God, infuses him with guilt and shame, redirects his steps, pushes closeness with his wife away, invades his thought life, and creates a curiosity for more. What a man thinks about the most he will eventually do (see Proverbs 23:7). Porn use brings with it the likelihood of depression and loneliness.

28. Pornography is a gateway to other sexual sins.

Pornography opens the door to other sexual sins such as visiting strip clubs, sex shops, prostitutes, exhibitionism, bondage-submission, voyeurism, phone sex, incest, and associated perversions, viewing child pornography, abuse, and rape.

A Christian man who initially looks at pornography would never dream that one day he would be paying for sex with a prostitute. The news is filled daily with such sad events. A pastor, who succumbed to the temptation of clicking the mouse and opening that porn site one day, would never have thought he would one day be photographed coming out of a strip club. A loving dad who detests anyone who would harm children could never believe that one day he would be viewing child pornography. Such is the blinding nature of pornography. "Pornography offers the path to a door that opens into a prison," writes Robert Jensen, in *Getting Off*.

29. Pornography destroys intimacy between husband and wife.

When a Christian man views pornography, emotional distance is created between himself and his wife. She may not know why there is distance, but it is obvious that intimacy is missing.

"One inescapable [aspect] of engaging in porn and lust is that a wall is immediately built between our wives and us; whether we feel it, acknowledge it or not," writes Stuart Vogelman, in "Does Porn or a Husband's Wandering Eyes Hurt a Marriage?" "Porn decreases your interest in a real relationship and increases your appetite for more porn" (fightthenewdrug .org/Get-The-Facts).

According to sociologist Jill Manning, research indicates pornography consumption is associated with the following six trends, among others:

- Increased marital distress and risk of separation and divorce
- Decreased marital intimacy and sexual satisfaction
- Infidelity
- Increased appetite for more graphic types of pornography and sexual activity associated with abusive, illegal, or unsafe practices
- Devaluation of monogamy, marriage and child rearing
- An increasing number of people struggling with compulsive and addictive sexual behavior

30. Pornography creates unrealistic expectations.

Pornography is unreal and creates unrealistic expectations of a man toward his wife and toward the activities that he attempts to emulate. This results in dissatisfaction within the marriage relationship. Pornography lies to a man and suggests that a normal sex life is like what is seen in the images, where women are always available and anything goes so long as it satisfies the man. This goes against everything the Bible teaches about the marriage relationship of unconditional love and sacrifice (Ephesians 5:25, 28). "A Utah University study found that regular porn use creates longings and needs that are rarely met in real life relationships."

31. Pornography in the home will be discovered by the children.

Your child discovering pornography if it is in your home or on your computer is not a matter of *if* but *when*. They will find it and when they do, it will be destructive. If their dad has pornography, they will assume it is acceptable.

On the Web site Dads.org, Steve Wood, a Catholic leader, effectively communicates the desperate situation regarding fathers and pornography:

The venom of Internet pornography is slowly killing the spiritual life of millions of Christian fathers. In the words of Jerry Kirk, pornography is "anti-children, anti-women, anti-marriage, anti-family, anti-church and anti-God." I add that pornography is profoundly anti-fatherhood. Nothing less than the future of Christian fatherhood is at stake in this battle for purity.

32. Pornography harms children.

Children are harmed emotionally when they see pornography. That image is there forever. As stated earlier, 90 percent of children aged 8 to 16 have viewed porn, and they have become the pornography industry's core target. Children who are habitually exposed to pornography will have sexual intercourse earlier and run the risk of developing an addiction.

In addition, pornography drives the demand for child pornography, victimizes innocent children, and the industry, desiring consumers for life, attempts to hook them on pornography at an early age.

Research reported in 2013 that child pornography is increasing; "between 2005–2009 there was a 432% increase in child pornography movies and images," according to pornharmsresearch.com.

Sexual predators surf the Internet in an attempt to solicit sex with children and teens. Witherspoon Institute's report, "The Social Costs of Pornography," points out:

> There is evidence that the prevalence of pornography in the lives of many children and adolescents is far more significant than most adults realize, that pornography is deforming the healthy sexual development of these young viewers, and that it is used to exploit children and adolescents.

33. Pornography increases the likelihood of a real-time affair.

Social Science Quarterly reported in, "Adult Social Bonds and Use of Internet Pornography," "One nationally representative study of 531 Internet users published in 2004 found that those who had had an extramarital affair were more than three times more likely to have used Internet pornography than were Internet users who had not had an affair. According to the same study, people who had engaged in paid sex or prostitution were almost four times more likely to have used Internet pornography than those who had not engaged in paid sex." Others report at fightthenewdrug.org: "Pornography use increases the marital infidelity rate by more than 300%."

There is a much shorter step to physical adultery once a man has habitually viewed pornography. Pornography encourages men to think about having sex outside their marriage. Beatriz Mileham, University of Florida, remarked, "The Internet will soon become the most common form of infidelity, if it is not already."

34. Pornography leads to divorce.

Habitually viewing pornography can become a reason for divorce. Since marriage is built on trust and that trust is broken through pornography use, if trust cannot be restored and repentance is not real, divorce becomes a possibility.

One huge question for Christians is, "If pornography viewing is adultery, does that give me permission to divorce, since adultery is the biblical grounds for divorce?" There is much discussion and much disagreement on that. As in a real affair, divorce is permissible by the innocent party, but it is *not commanded*. There can be restoration if the offending party is willing to demonstrate the fruits of repentance. It is my interpretation that the same applies to pornography viewing. Yes, it's that serious.

At a 2003 meeting of the American Academy of Matrimonial Lawyers, two thirds of the 350 divorce lawyers who attended said the Internet played a significant role in their divorce cases in the past year, with excessive interest in online porn contributing to more than half such cases. Pornography had an almost nonexistent role in divorce just seven or eight years prior to that, according to Divorcewizards.com. Imagine what that number would be today.

35. Pornography at work is an increasing problem.

Seventy percent of all online porn access occurs during the 9:00 to 5:00 workday, which leads us to conclude that much of that access is taking place while at work. Twenty percent of men and 13 percent of women admitted to accessing pornography at work. Two thirds of 500 human resources professionals polled said they have found pornography on their employees' computers. Businesses, organizations, ministries, and churches are having to install software to protect their employees and their integrity.

In the church I have pastored since 1996, we have had to dismiss staff members for viewing pornography and sending inappropriate sexual emails. Filters add one more layer of protection to help prevent clicking on porn sites.

36. There are more than 101 different subcategories of pornography.

If a sexual scene or activity can be imagined, the porn industry can create it through an image. There are categories based on age, physical appearance, hair color, body features, skin color, as well as on fetishes (sexual stimulation through an object or specific activity). Most of these are hardcore. Satan has designed a pornographic image, scene, or activity for any temptation. Undoubtedly there will be new genres created as this addiction to pornography increases.

37. Viewing pornography is sin.

A Christian simply cannot view pornography and not sin. It is not possible. Why? Pornography creates lust and lust is sin. Pornography cannot be justified for any reason in the life of a child of God. The following verses teach that porn viewing is sin:

> *You have heard that it was said, 'You shall not commit adultery.'*
> *But I tell you that anyone who looks at a woman lustfully has*
> *committed adultery with her already in his heart.*
> — Matthew 5:27–28 (NIV)

For all that is in the world, the lust of the flesh and the lust of the eyes and the boastful pride of life, is not from the Father, but is from the world.

—1 John 2:16

Now the deeds of the flesh are evident, which are: immorality, impurity, sensuality.

— Galatians 5:19

Abstain from every form of evil.

— 1 Thessalonians 5:22 (ESV)

The one who commits adultery with a woman is lacking sense; he who would destroy himself does it. Wounds and disgrace he will find.

— Proverbs 6:32–33

But among you there must not be even a hint of sexual immorality or of any kind of impurity, or of greed, because these are improper for God's holy people. . . . For of this you can be sure: No immoral, impure or greedy person—such a person is an idolater—has any inheritance in the kingdom of Christ and of God.

—Ephesians 5:3, 5 (NIV)

38. Pornography is a drug.

Pornography is the drug of choice for many men, in an attempt to medicate their wounds and pain from the past and the stress and pressure of the present. That's why Kastleman calls pornography "the drug of the new millennium" because it alters the brain.

Brain images have shown that continued exposure to pornography has the same kind of effect on the brain as a drug like cocaine. In the book

Hyperstimulation: Teens, Porn and Online Addictions, the authors state: "When engaged in cybersex the dopamine level in a teen's brain increases 1100%. Dopamine is considered the feel-good chemical." Some experts report that it's easier to break a heroin addiction than it is to break a sexual addiction.

Mary Anne Layden, codirector of the Sexual Trauma and Psychopathology Program at the University of Pennsylvania's Center for Cognitive Therapy, called porn the "most concerning thing to psychological health that I know of existing today."

Layden said, "The Internet is a perfect drug delivery system because you are anonymous, aroused and have role models for these behaviors. . . To have [a] drug pumped into your house 24/7, free, and children know how to use it better than grown-ups know how to use it—it's a perfect delivery system if we want to have a whole generation of young addicts who will never have the drug out of their mind."

"Pornography addicts have a more difficult time recovering from their addiction than cocaine addicts, since coke users can get the drug out of their system, but pornographic images stay in the brain forever" (wired.com).

39. Pornography elicits acting out.

Pornography elicits an action of some type. The most common form of acting out while viewing pornography is masturbation. Masturbation can easily become enslaving. If a man continues his pornography habit, sinful actions will follow. On the Web site womenfordecency.org, we read:

> It typically starts out with occasionally looking at pictures of scantily dressed people and then progresses from soft-core to hard-core pornography. This progression can lead to acting out behaviors such as online and in-person emotional and sexual affairs, visiting strip clubs, soliciting prostitutes, child pornography, sexual abuse of self or others, exhibitionism, voyeurism, rape, and sex in the context of violence.

"There is an abundant amount of evidence that shows viewers of pornography often seek to find ways to perform in real life the same certain sex acts that they saw on films, magazines and online" (pornharmsresearch.com).

40. Pornography encourages premarital and extramarital sex.

Those who use pornography disregard the biblical teaching that sex should be reserved for marriage and, once married, should be exclusive within that marriage.

Paul Wright, PhD, at Indiana University concludes that men who regularly view pornography are more likely to engage in casual sex, have multiple partners, and cheat on their spouse.

There are numerous Scriptures that declare sex before marriage to be a sin: Acts 15:20; 1 Corinthians 5:1; 6:13, 18; 10:8; 2 Corinthians 12:21; Galatians 5:19; Ephesians 5:3; Colossians 3:5; 1 Thessalonians 4:3; Jude 7; Hebrews 13:4. There is no moral standard in pornography; it is anything goes sexually regardless of marital status. Pornography affects the beliefs, attitudes, and morals of those who continually watch it. One's moral wall is lowered and what was off-limits sexually becomes acceptable.

41. Pornography suggests that sex is a man's greatest need.

Sex is not man's greatest need. An intimate relationship with God and then, if married, with his wife is his greatest need. Sex alone never fills the void within a Christian man's life. Pornography leaves a man empty, shame-filled, and guilt-ridden. Intimacy with God and his wife never makes a man feel that way; it brings fulfillment on a level that pornography could never offer. When a Christian man looks to pornography, he is not searching for sex; he is looking for *intimacy*.

42. Pornography feeds sex trafficking.

Sex trafficking is the use of humans against their will—a multitude of them being children or young teens—for the purpose of paid sexual activity. They are sex slaves used to bring sexual pleasure, primarily to men.

Although most Christian men would never affirm that activity, there are clear connections between pornography and sex trafficking. In "The Connections Between Pornography and Sex Trafficking" Ana Stutler wrote:

> This dichotomy between sex trafficking and the realities of pornography is a serious misconception that needs to be addressed. As individuals who seek to oppose sex trafficking, we must understand its linkage to pornography. . . how pornography drives demand for sex trafficking, how victims of trafficking are used in the production of pornography, and [how] the production of pornography constitutes sex trafficking under current legal definitions (covenanteyes.com).

43. Pornography is becoming normalized and acceptable in society.

Thirty-eight percent of adults say porn is morally acceptable. That number will continue to rise. This is affecting Christians too. Society is becoming "pornified," accepting pornography as normal, and acceptable. While some believe that men looking at porn is just men being men, it is apparent that things that once shocked us are now being accepted as normal in our society. Our society is losing its ability to blush (see Jeremiah 6:15). One can only imagine what will be acceptable on prime-time television within ten years.

Christians must decide now how they will protect their minds and hearts and how they will respond to the sexualized media and pornography beforehand. Waiting to respond until after those images are seen is too late. A battle plan for responding to sinful thoughts should be in place before that image is seen. The sexualized media and pornography are not going away, so it becomes essential for Christians to equip themselves in advance, to know how they will respond in a godly way.

44. Pornography violates a wife's right to have a husband who belongs exclusively to her.

Paul makes it clear that a wife's body belongs to her husband and equally a husband's body belongs to his wife (1 Corinthians 7:4). They are exclusive domains physically, emotionally, and relationally. When a husband gives his eyes, attention, focus, and passion to someone (albeit an image) that is not his wife, he has violated this principle. This is not an issue of one spouse trying to control the other, but one of mutual respect, love, and unconditional giving to your spouse.

A Christian marriage is one where the other person's happiness trumps your own. Pornography only focuses on *me*. A spouse has every right to expect exclusive love and attention. The spouse who views pornography invites an unwelcome third person into the marriage.

45. Pornography affects Christian men from every background.

While pornography especially attracts Christian men who have been abused or abandoned and those who have been exposed to it early, it does not play favorites (see XXXchurch.com). Christian men from every walk of life and profession are affected by the pornography plague. From doctors to factory workers; politicians to welders; lawyers to sanitation workers; CEO's to restaurant cooks; millionaires to those on welfare; policemen to prisoners; school teachers to musicians; pastors to priests; educated to noneducated—pornography is prevalent. There is no Christian man who could say, "Sexual sin cannot happen to me." Christian men's conference leader Bill Perkins said concerning Christian men: "If you think you cannot fall into sexual sin, then you're godlier than David, stronger than Samson, and wiser than Solomon." ("Why Filtered Internet," American Family Online, afo.net).

46. Pornography is becoming the new sex education tool.

Sadly, many young men are getting their sex education through Internet pornography sites and scenes. Sociologist Diana Russell, who has written several books on the subject of Web porn's influence on children, claims: "Unfortunately for many kids growing up today, pornography is the only sex education they'll get."

What is seen on porn sites becomes normal behavior in the minds of those who watch it, especially young men who have not been told the facts of life from a biblical worldview or even from a moral viewpoint. Imagine what young women will face in the future because of pornography's influence!

Researchers at the University of Montreal wanted to compare the behavior of men who viewed sexually explicit material with those who had never looked at it all. But professor Simon Louis Lajeunesse says he had to drastically rethink his study after failing to find any male volunteers who had never viewed porn. The study had to be scrapped (dailymail.co.uk/news/article).

47. Pornography presents the idea of sexual sin with no consequences.

Most younger people and some adults seem to think that they are immune from the consequences of looking at pornography. It certainly never communicates the consequences of sex with anyone, anytime, anywhere. In the fantasy porn world, women never get pregnant, and men never get a sexually transmitted infection or disease. HIV appears not to be a possibility. Real-world issues such as menstrual cycles, illness, children's needs, exhaustion, fear, worry, or money problems are nonexistent in the porn industry's presentation of sex.

The possibility of abuse is never considered. Pornography is communicating to a generation that sex outside of marriage never has negative consequences and always brings pleasure. Porn has encouraged the "hook-up" philosophy of sex without commitments. Yet God's Word says, "Do not be deceived: God cannot be mocked. A man reaps what he sows. Whoever sows to please their flesh, from the flesh will reap destruction; whoever sows to please the Spirit, from the Spirit will reap eternal life" (Galatians 6:7–8 NIV).

48. Pornography enslavement can be overcome.

In the power of a resurrected Savior, anyone can break free from the chains of pornography, get beyond moral failure, and experience God's grace, with His healing and forgiveness. But it doesn't happen without repentance, brokenness, and faith. Overcoming a pornography struggle or habit is a process, not a quick fix. Whether it is your husband, son, or fiancé, or the spouse or son of a friend who is struggling with pornography, there are seven questions, based on John 8:1–11, that a person must work through. He needs to be able to respond positively to the following seven questions in order to experience forgiveness and healing from sexual sin, specifically the sin of viewing pornography:

- Are you fully ready to deal with your pornography viewing as sin and repent?
- Are you willing to run to God and not away from Him and His will anymore?
- Are you willing to take total responsibility for your sexual brokenness because of your viewing pornography?
- Are you willing to admit your powerlessness over pornography and lust?
- Do you believe God can and will forgive you?
- Are you willing to do whatever it takes to repair your life story?
- Are you willing to forgive yourself once God forgives you?

49. The best defense in your home against pornography requires four realities. The best way to protect your home against pornography is by constantly working on four areas:

A CLOSE FAMILY LIFE—spending time together, having fun together, praying together, attending church together, laughing together, ministering together, and studying the Bible together.

A GOOD MARRIAGE—constantly working on having a godly and growing marriage, realizing your marriage is always under construction, and making the Bible your marriage manual.

A GOOD RELATIONSHIP BETWEEN PARENTS AND CHILDREN— working on communicating with each other, listening, seeking to understand each other, and being available to each other.

A DELIBERATE PARENTAL MONITORING OF INTERNET USE—
using Internet filtering and accountability software, setting
clear boundaries for Internet and cell phone use, and enforcing
those boundaries (Patrick Fagan, "The Effects of Pornography
on Individuals, Marriage, Family and Community," frc.org).

50. Pornography is increasingly becoming a problem for women, including Christian women.

Although the percentage of those viewing pornography is 70 percent men
and 30 percent women, it is increasingly becoming a problem for women,
even Christian women. In 2003, *Today's Christian Woman* reported that 34
percent of female readers of its online newsletter admitted to intentionally accessing Internet porn. Nineteen percent of Christian and teen girls
admitted they were not just exposed to it; they were addicted. And, of
those who say they were exposed to pornography, 44 percent said they felt
hopeless in overcoming it.

Craig Gross, founder of XXXchurch.com, told the *Christian Post* that
porn for men is a "quick, easy and satisfying" venture; while for women,
it's more of an escape. Also, men tend to be more visual; while for
women, emotional intimacy is involved. Thus, women tend to struggle
on a different level, and they later have conflicts when it comes to sex
and relationships.

Two good Web sites to help women who are struggling with pornography are DirtyGirlsMinistries.com and BeggarsDaughter.com.

Let these 50 thoughts show you how pervasive and dangerous pornography is and challenge you to fight the battle for a pornography-free home
and marriage. You can also spread the word to the leaders in your church,
asking them to challenge men to make the *Our Hardcore Battle Plan* commitment and Join 1 Million Men, committing themselves to live a porn-
free life.

How Should You Respond?

5

How should a Christian woman respond to the plague of pornography? With pornography affecting every home and church, godly women will be the key to change.

How can you communicate with your pastor(s) your concern that the issue of pornography in the pew needs to be addressed?

How can you help another woman who is struggling with the discovery that her husband, even though he is a Christian, is using pornography?

What can you do to help the men in your life—your husband or your son, to avoid pornography?

How can you pray for your husband, your son, for the men in the church you attend, or for the husbands of friends?

And this is where it gets extremely personal: What should you do if you discover that your husband or your son has been viewing pornography?

As we gathered the women in the church I pastor for a time of addressing these issues, there was weeping, relief, confession, testimonies of breakthroughs, heartbreaking stories of pain, and a resolve to address the issue and change its impact. There is a hunger among Christian women to win this battle for the minds and souls of their husbands and sons.

There has to be a firm conviction that we must never concede that Satan has won, that pornography is unbeatable. Out of this conviction we began an emphasis on challenging 1 million Christian women praying for 1 million men to live pornography-free lives.

As a pastor, I have experienced for years the power of godly, praying women to change things. "The prayer of a person living right with God is something powerful to be reckoned with" (James 5:16 *The Message*).

Because of pornography's four powerful hooks—accessibility, anonymity, affordability, addiction—every spiritual weapon you possess must be utilized in this battle.

God's Standard for Healthy Sex

Before looking at how to address the pornography issue, we need to be reminded of God's standard for healthy sex. Once we understand God's design for sex, we can more easily see how pornography and its effects pervert that standard.

Many in the pornography industry would have us believe that God is antisex. Nothing could be further from the truth. God created sex and gave it to married couples as a wonderful, pleasurable, intimate gift. Pornography presents sex as a physical act only, yet God presents sex as involving a person's spiritual and emotional life as well as the physical. As we understand God's standard for healthy sex, we will be able to help others, especially those who are being affected by pornography and its consequences. Further, this helps us to know what is acceptable and unacceptable in sex; questions whose answers are muddled by pornography.

With the prevalence of Internet pornography and other increasingly sexualized media, many husbands are asking their wives to do sexual acts that may be uncomfortable or demeaning. Let's clarify what is acceptable and not acceptable when it comes to sexual practices.

Now regarding the questions you asked in your letter. Yes, it is good to abstain from sexual relations. But because there is so much sexual immorality, each man should have his own wife, and each woman should have her own husband.

The husband should fulfill his wife's sexual needs, and the wife should fulfill her husband's needs. The wife gives authority over her body to her husband, and the husband gives authority over his body to his wife.

Do not deprive each other of sexual relations, unless you both agree to refrain from sexual intimacy for a limited time so you can give yourselves more completely to prayer. Afterward, you should come together again so that Satan won't be able to tempt you because of your lack of self-control.
—1 Corinthians 7:1–5 (NLT)

From these verses we can identify four major principles of healthy and acceptable sex.

Healthy Sex Is Married Sex

But because of immoralities, each man is to have his own wife, and each woman is to have her own husband (1 Corinthians 7:2).

Love is not the boundary for sex, marriage is—and only marriage. The media most often portrays sex outside of marriage as exciting and adventurous, while sex within marriage is portrayed as boring, dull, and humdrum—just the opposite of God's reality. This is underscored by the following 2008 report from the Parents Television Council:

Sex in the context of marriage is either nonexistent on primetime broadcast television, or is depicted as burdensome rather than as an expression of love and commitment. By contrast, extramarital or adulterous sexual relationships are depicted with greater frequency, and overwhelmingly as a positive experience. Across the broadcast networks, verbal references to nonmarital sex outnumbered references to sex in the context of marriage by nearly 3 to 1; and scenes depicting or implying sex between nonmarried partners outnumbered scenes depicting or implying sex between married partners by a ratio of nearly 4 to 1.

Pornography puts absolutely no credence on sex in marriage. The portrayal on porn sites is most often between unmarried people. And as has been mentioned and documented thoroughly, many of these are trafficked peoples. Others are desperate individuals who are preying on others for their own gain, with complete disregard for Jesus Christ and His followers.

Pornography promotes sex outside of marriage. Walt Larimore, reporting in a survey at imom.com, confirms that the greatest and most satisfying sexual experience is between a man and his wife within the boundaries of marriage.

Healthy Sex Is Regular Sex

> *Stop depriving one another, except by agreement for a time, so that you may devote yourselves to prayer, and come together again so that Satan will not tempt you because of your lack of self-control.*
>
> —1 Corinthians 7:5

Paul places an exception clause in abstaining from sex within marriage. Abstinence is permissible for a period of time if you both agree to it, and if it is for the purpose of prayer and fasting. The idea is when there is an issue so pressing and urgent that both of you agree, that instead of having sex for a short period of time, you may each give yourself to prayer and seeking God.

Then come back together again. Satan has an ingenious way of tempting us when we least expect it. Sex is never to be used as a weapon or a reward. "Stop depriving" (1 Corinthians 7:5) means don't rob each other, don't keep a distance, don't withhold.

If you do continue to abstain from sexual relations, temptation is certain to come. Prolonged sexual abstinence among married people creates welcome mats for Satan's temptations. As Cathy Dyer believes, "In the majority of marriages, the man desires sex more often than the woman. Recognize that, and try to at least meet him in the middle."

Healthy Sex Is Unselfish Sex

> *The husband must fulfill his duty to his wife, and likewise also the wife to her husband. The wife does not have authority over her own body, but the husband does; and likewise also the husband does not have authority over his own body, but the wife does* (1 Corinthians 7:3–4).

Marriage is a decision to serve the other, both in the bedroom and outside of it. Duty means a debt, a responsibility. It means to give sexual satisfaction to each other. In other words you are responsible to meet each other's needs sexually. Husbands and wives have the same rights when it comes to sex.

Paul teaches that the husband and wife release the authority of their bodies over to the other. Within marriage there is everything needed to fulfill sexual needs. Married couples owe each other sexual happiness. The goal in sex between husband and wife is to please each other, not seek self-satisfaction first. The husband and wife are responsible to please each other sexually.

Healthy Sex Is Loving Sex

Loving refers to gentleness, tenderness, patience, and kindness toward your marriage partner in the sexual experience. Sex is not demanded; it is given in the context of unconditional love, that is described in 1 Corinthians 13.

> *Love is patient, love is kind and is not jealous; love does not brag and is not arrogant, does not act unbecomingly; it does not seek its own, is not provoked, does not take into account a wrong suffered, does not rejoice in unrighteousness, but rejoices with the truth; bears all things, believes all things, hopes all things, endures all things. Love never fails* (vv. 4–8).

Rights and responsibilities to each other are different from demanding from each other. Healthy sex does not insist that the marriage partner do things that are uncomfortable emotionally, spiritually, or physically. There should be an agreement between the two spouses regarding what is acceptable and within the boundaries of comfort and security.

If you are uncomfortable with certain aspects or acts of sex, communicate that to your husband. God's standard never injures, intentionally inflicts pain, demands demeaning acts, or demonstrates rudeness, violence, or doing anything against your will.

Each couple must decide for themselves in the Spirit of Jesus what is appropriate for them. There should be no violation of each other's comfort zone or conscience. Should married couples be creative? Yes, but not at the expense of making the other feel uncomfortable.

The takeaway from these verses is, any sexual practice, activity, suggestion, request, or portrayal of sex that is not consistent with these principles, is out of bounds for a Christian.

With that in mind, I shared with the women in our church a teaching on "What Every Man Wishes His Wife Knew About Sex." May I tell you that it was very awkward and a bit embarrassing for me to share these things? However, the response was very encouraging. I communicated "What Does My Husband Want from Me When It Comes to Sex?" in a list from A to Z. But this list doesn't in any way suggest that if a woman's husband is struggling with pornography that his wife is to blame. These were simply some suggestions to take away some of the power of Satan's temptations. Please keep that in mind.

Those who are single or choose to remain single must wrestle with what Scripture makes clear. Looking at the life of Jesus Christ is a wonderful place to start.

A Man's Greatest Need

Men find it easier to believe that sex is everything and that more sex is the total answer to all problems. Your husband's greatest need is *not* sex, but for intimacy with God, and with you. For most men, however, intimacy with you is spelled S-E-X.

*A*ppeal to the eyes—Men are affected by what they see.

*B*e his best friend.

*C*ompliment him—Find something he is doing right and let him know about it.

*D*on't use sex as a weapon by giving it as a reward or withholding it as a punishment.

*E*steem him—Let him know you respect him and admire him.

*F*lirt with him—In private and in public.

*G*ive him something to anticipate sexually.

*H*elp him with those areas where he struggles without making him feel like he is inadequate.

*I*nitiate sex sometimes.

*J*oin him in pursuing his dreams and goals.

*L*et him know you believe in him and will do everything possible to help him fulfill his dreams and goals.

*K*now the things that make him happy and do your best to do them.

*L*ook your best—inside and out. He was attracted to you when you met; your spirit, and physical person. He will be attracted to you now as you continue to be at *your* very best.

*M*ake sex a priority. It certainly is to him.

*N*eglect not your husband's sexual needs.

*O*ffer to take some burden from him and make it your project.

*P*ut-downs are turn-offs whether in private or public.

*Q*uestion daily; "What can I do to help him to find happiness?"

*R*ecreation with him is important. Learn to enjoy the things he enjoys.

*S*pecifically tell him your needs. Sometimes men just don't get it. That means sexual needs too. Don't be embarrassed or shy. He may never know unless you spell it out for him.

*T*hank him for the things he does that provide for you and your family.

*U*nderstand his need for private time and relaxation. When you and he get home, you may be emotionally and physically spent. Give each other some space to unwind. He may not want to immediately relive his whole day with specific details.

*V*ulnerability to sexual sin can be lessened by the things you do. Christian psychologist Kevin Leman says, "A sexually fulfilled husband will do anything for you."*

*W*ork on ways to keep the fun and excitement in your marriage.

*eX*amine your attitude. Ask yourself, "Am I being too hard, or critical, or am I nagging?"

*Y*awn not—Don't act bored with your husband. Be interested in him.

*Z*ip your lips at appropriate times. There are times, especially in those intimate moments, when you don't need to bring up issues.

* Please do remember that if your husband is struggling with pornography, this is his decision and in no way can be justified by how much or how little sex he is experiencing with you.

Approaching Your Husband About the Issue of Pornography

Approaching him in no way suggests that your husband is struggling with viewing pornography; however, this does open the door for discussion and for protection in the future.

At an appropriate time (sooner is better than later), sit down with your husband and have this discussion. There are three specific questions you need to ask your husband. Set the time and create an atmosphere free of stress, time constraints, and distractions. Before you ask these three questions, make sure you have prepared your own heart and mind.

Pray and seek God's wisdom. Learn about preparing for spiritual warfare (found in Ephesians 6:10–18). Satan will put up a fight when dealing with issues of marital intimacy. Also ask a friend you trust to pray for you.

Your husband's answers may be reassuring and encouraging, however, it is possible, given the number of men involved in pornography, that the answers you receive may be wounding and painful. If you discover that your husband is viewing pornography, realize that this is *not* your fault! Don't let Satan lie to you and suggest that you don't measure up or that you are not appealing enough. This is not about you; it is about your husband's sinful choices and actions.

Understanding why and how Satan tempts your husband is essential to helping him. As we gathered the women of our church on a Wednesday evening, Cathy Dyer shared with them some of what she had learned from her experience:

> Understand that most men do not seek out pornography
> because of something their wife is or isn't doing; rather, they

seek it out because Satan has tailored it to their wiring. It was meant to ensnare and manipulate them. Just like a good sale sign lures us into our favorite store, pornography is alluring because it speaks directly to the visual wiring of a man's mind. It is truly every man's battle. . . . Pornography is a vicious animal that gets its talons into a man's mind where you cannot reach. You can want your husband to quit and love him with all that is in you, but if he doesn't commit in his heart to kick the habit, it's not going to happen.

So what are the three questions you should ask your husband?

1.   Am I meeting your needs physically/sexually?

Ask this to open the door for discussion. He may initially dismiss it and not want to talk about it, but assure him you genuinely want to know and that his answer will not cause an argument.

2.   What can I do to help you sexually?

Give your husband an opportunity to specifically share with you things you could do that would help him. Ask him to be specific with you. Let him know how he can meet your needs sexually.

3.   Are you struggling with pornography?

Assure him that you need to know so that, if he is, you can know how to help him with this struggle. Viewing pornography is never right; in fact it is sinful. However, admitting it is the first step of healing. You have every right to be angry if the answer is yes. But you must deal with your anger in a godly way.

What If You Discover That Your Husband Is Viewing Pornography?

As you can tell by reading Cathy Dyer's chapters in this book, a woman who discovers her husband is using pornography (or has gone to the next step and committed both spiritual and physical adultery) experiences an emotional roller coaster. Obviously, if your husband admits to viewing pornography, you will feel betrayed, hurt, angry, embarrassed, and violated. And you have every right to be angry. Trust has been broken. You feel devalued and disrespected.

Then insecurity makes you wonder, *Why aren't I enough for him?* Remember that you are *not* the reason he looked at pornography.

You are probably beginning to connect the dots as to why your husband seemed so distant, almost like a stranger at times. You feel embarrassed and rejected. You worry that there is more: if your husband looked at pornography, what else has he done? If you have children, you worry that they may have discovered it too.

A thousand questions and emotions stir in your mind and heart. You wonder what or who was on his mind when you were having sex. Things are beginning to make more sense now as to why your husband went into sexual overdrive, wanting more sex—or the opposite, the reason he developed a seeming disinterest in sex. Perhaps you now understand why your husband asked you to do things that were uncomfortable for you. You wonder if he is looking at other women or even if he has had an affair.

No doubt you feel fear about the future and have many questions about the past.

- *When did my husband start looking at porn?*
- *How often did he view it?*
- *Does he truly love me?*
- *Why did he feel a need to find sexual excitement outside of our relationship?*
- *Life as we knew it has changed because of my husband's choice. How committed is he to this marriage?*
- *What do I do now? How do I go forward from this point?*
- *Should I demand my husband leave?*
- *Should I go to marriage counseling?*
- *Should I demand my husband go to counseling, join a support group, get into an accountability group?*

These are all issues that need to be addressed. Let's look at them in detail.

1. Communicate with your husband exactly how you feel.

You may be literally speechless after your husband confesses to using pornography. If so, after you have had a chance to think things through, you will need to have this conversation with him. When you do, hold back *nothing*.

Express your feelings of disrespect, betrayal, and anger. Let him know how his choice to view pornography has affected you emotionally and spiritually. Be totally transparent and specific. This will be cathartic for you and show him how much damage he has done to your marriage. Share with him exactly how his viewing pornography has made you feel as a woman. Righteous anger is totally acceptable, although there is a fine line between righteous anger and sin. Paul said in Ephesians 4:26, "Be angry, and yet do not sin." But be angry without sinning against God, yourself, your husband, and others.

2. Ask him if he has repented.

God will forgive. His grace gives new beginnings.

Real repentance means more than being sorry he got caught. Repentance is a change of heart that leads to a change of behavior. "Produce fruit in keeping with repentance" (Matthew 3:8). Without repentance and brokenness over sin, there is no change. Only repentance can start the cycle of breaking the bondage to pornography. Repentance means he has experienced an overwhelming sense of sorrow for what he has done, and he vows in God's power to never again look at pornography. If he has not truly repented, he will probably not be willing to follow through on the other steps.

3. Insist that all pornography in his possession be eliminated now.

You have a right to know where, when, and how your husband was viewing pornography. All porn stashes must be destroyed, no exceptions. Is there any porn downloaded on his computer? It may be necessary for the computer hard drive to be wiped clean. Premium cable that carries X-rated material must be eliminated if he is serious about living a pornography-free life. And there's more.

4. Demand that he get into a support group.

Your husband will not experience healing by himself. He must be in a group that will hold him accountable and weekly make him face the reality of what he has done and the price to get back what was lost. There are issues in his life that created his drive to look at pornography and these need to be addressed. There may be past abuse or abandonment issues that he has never confronted. Determine if there is a support group in the church that he can attend. If not, have him to find one in a local church or Christian ministry.

5. Insist that he immediately ask other Christian men for accountability.

Ask him to write down the names of at least five men that he could meet with on a regular basis for accountability. Put a specific time limit on when this is to be accomplished.

These men should be godly and mature men whom your husband respects and could call at any hour of the day or night if he is triggered to think about looking at pornography. You cannot be your husband's accountability partner. That is not your job. You can support him in ways no one else can, however, true accountability needs to happen outside your relationship.

Your husband may need to go through therapy with a credible, Christian psychologist to address root issues from his past. In addition, he may need to attend an intensive weekend to begin the breaking-free process. One of the most effective workshop's for men is led by Mark Laaser, founder of Faithful and True Ministries, faithfulandtrue.com.

6. Have Internet accountability and blocking software installed on every computer and cell phone.

Both are necessary. Covenant Eyes provides both and is very effective. This is a must, to create one more wall to hinder him ever looking at pornography again. You can go to covenanteyes.com and see how this works. Also XXXchurch.com has an effective software program called X3WatchPRO, an online accountability filter. From Covenant Eye's Web site they differentiate between accountability and filtering software:

> Our Internet Accountability software monitors how the Internet is used and sends a report to the person you select, such as a friend, parent or mentor. This online transparency helps you think twice about how you use the Web. Our Internet filtering software lets you set time limits and block Web sites based on age—and customizable parental controls for each of your kids.

7. **Ask your husband to go to your pastor or a spiritual leader to confess what he has done.**
Although he will be meeting with other Christian men for accountability, to fully come clean he needs to confess his failure to your pastor or a Christian leader in the church you attend. James says, "Therefore confess your sins to each other, and pray for each other so that you may be healed" (James 5:16 NIV). This is an important step in your husband's healing. He needs to set up the appointment and then tell you about it once he has met with a pastor.

8. **Outline for him what it is going to take to build back the trust he has broken.**
List what it will take for you to trust him again. Be specific, such as him giving you his password, letting you check his phone and his computer at any time, calling you during the day to check in, and being willing to answer the question, "Have you looked at pornography today?" He must agree to do these things without becoming angry or dismissive of the need for them. This step is vital and must be communicated clearly.

9. **Draw up boundaries and define consequences.**
Clearly and specifically communicate with your husband the consequences if he continues to view pornography. Share with him the boundaries of what is acceptable to you and what is not acceptable. Cathy Dyer's

husband, Greg, said concerning the consequences of his pornography habit, "A man isn't going to take it seriously until something is on the line." I would even encourage putting boundaries in writing.

10. Pour out to God and a trusted friend your feelings.

You can pour out all your feelings of anger, jealousy, betrayal, and hurt to God. Hold nothing back. You can talk as loudly as you need to; God understands. The worst thing you could do is to stop talking to God. You desperately need Him. The psalmists reminds us that God will listen as you cry out:

> *The righteous cry, and the Lord hears*
> *And delivers them out of all their troubles.*
> *The Lord is near to the brokenhearted*
> *And saves those who are crushed in spirit.*
>
> —Psalm 34:17–18

> *Cast your burden upon the Lord and He will sustain you;*
> *He will never allow the righteous to be shaken.*
>
> —Psalm 55:22

Other references: Psalm 37:5, 24; 112:6

Then find at least one trusted friend that you can confide in, someone who loves you unconditionally and will be there for you and walk with you through this difficult journey. "Form your purpose by asking for counsel, then carry it out using all the help you can get" (Proverbs 20:18 *The Message*).

11. Ask specific questions.

Even if part of you feels as if you'd rather not know, there are some questions your husband needs to answer. For trust to be rebuilt, your husband needs to come totally clean with you. You have every right to ask these questions:

- Has he ever had an affair?
- At any time has he visited adult businesses, strip clubs, prostitutes, or had phone sex or any other type of cybersex?
- Has he had or is he having an emotional and/or physical affair with anyone?
- Does he have subscriptions to anything pornographic coming to the house, the office, or a rented post office box?
- Are there any other sinful secrets he is keeping from you?

While it may seem you are giving him the third degree, you are establishing a truth point with your husband. This is his opportunity to come totally clean. And although painful for both of you, if he is truthful, it is a place you should never have to revisit.

12. Care enough to check up.

Randomly check the history on his computer. He should have given you all his passwords. History erased on his computer is a red flag. Check those places where pornography has been hidden in the past. His willingness to do this is one way he can demonstrate his commitment to live a pornography-free life. Although these random checkups are needed, you cannot be his porn cop, taking responsibility for watching him all hours of the night and day. Getting and staying pornography-free must be his responsibility.

13. Pray, read the Bible, and journal.

Cathy Dyer, when struggling with her husband, who was hooked on pornography and involved in a sexual affair, shared that three things helped sustain her through this turbulent time. These three can do the same for you: prayer, reading God's Word, and writing down your thoughts, feelings, and insights as you walk through the valley of despair.

> These three things helped me get through some really rocky paths in that year of separation and counseling. It's cheap therapy! When I would cry tears of pain, I always prayed to God

through those tears. He became "Daddy" to me during that time. Often, I would write prayers to God and pour my heart out to Him, and sometimes, I got answers. Then there were the precious times when I would turn to a random passage and it would seem that a particular verse had a sunbeam shining on it. I would read it and break down, knowing that God had directed me to those very words. I kept a list of the verses I felt God had shown me; I call them my "Rainbow verses" (chap. 3 in this book.)

14. Be aware of his temptations (where he works, the people he works with, the people he spends the most time with).

Are there people with whom he works who concern you? Tell him. Are there influences where he works that would make it more difficult for him to keep his pornography-free commitment? Explore ways to address those moral and spiritual landmines. Share with him your vulnerabilities because of his choice to look at pornography.

Utilize good resources online those found in books.

There are helpful resources available to aid you through this process. Here are some suggestions on books and Web sites to assist you in your journey:

Recommended Books:

Healing the Wounds of Sexual Addiction, Mark Laaser

Shattered Vows, Debra Laaser

The Porn Trap, Wendy and Larry Maltz

Don't Call It Love, Patrick Carnes

In the Shadows of the Net, Patrick Carnes, David Delmonico, Elizabeth Griffin

When Good Men Are Tempted, Bill Perkins

Eyes of Integrity: The Porn Pandemic and How It Affects You, Craig Gross

The Drug of the New Millennium: The Brain Science Behind Internet Pornography Use, Mark B. Kastleman

Recommended Web sites:

PornHarms.org

Faithfulandtrueministries.com

XXXchurch.com

ThePinkCross.org

Healthysex.com

Bethesdaworkshops.org

Freedomeveryday.org (L.I.F.E. Ministries)

SA.org (Sexaholics Anonymous)

15. Decide when to resume normal sexual relations.

Although, after initially discovering his porn viewing you will not desire a sexual relationship with your husband, to withhold sex indefinitely while trying to sustain the marriage would create an even more difficult situation. He may find that this is even more of a temptation for himself. There should be a time where sex is halted, for the purpose of prayer for you and repentance and prayer for him.

But there has to be a time when normalcy returns. How soon you agree to resume marital relations should be conditioned on both his faithfulness in going through the steps to keep him clean of pornography and to regain your trust, and on your ability to come to terms with what has happened in your marriage and to forgive him. Both of these are a process, not a one-time, momentary event.

Think of what has happened to you as similar to having been in a car accident where "out of nowhere" (as Cathy said) a truck T-boned your side of the car. Imagine that your car was totaled and you sustained some fairly severe injuries. You spent a week in the hospital and came home with one leg in a cast and an arm in a sling. Only the most selfish and insensitive of husbands would demand sexual relations the night you returned home.

Discovering your husband's involvement with pornography—with or without the added injury of adultery—creates a type of wreckage in your marriage. With commitment on his part and time and the forgiveness that you can only give through Christ, you can have a strong marriage in the future. Cathy's story in this book is one example. But the severity of the problem should not be swept under the rug—or the bed—in a rush to make things seem as normal as possible at the crash scene.

Previously, the suggestion was made that your husband might need to see a counselor. It is also possible that you may need professional counseling. Especially if you find yourself slipping into depression over the situation, seek help from a professional, Christian counselor.

Keep in mind your comfort level. The level of harm can vary greatly, and the influence of porn—especially upon discovery of a problem, rather than as a preemptive strike—should be handled more delicately.

16. Ask him to take the Sexual Addiction Screening Test.

It is available at Sexhelp.com. Once he takes it, go over it together and discuss it. Ask him to share with you why he believes he struggles with pornography. Try to discover when your husband began struggling with pornography and how that has affected him. Often the seeds of the pornography struggle began when a person saw a sexual image at a young age.

17. Choose to forgive based on his repentance, but understand that forgiveness and trust are two different things.

Forgiveness is a choice one makes, not a feeling. My professor at Fuller Seminary, Dr. Arch Hart, shared the best definition of forgiveness I have ever heard. "Forgiveness is surrendering your right to hurt back someone who has hurt you." Yet forgiveness should not be offered prematurely. Your husband needs to demonstrate repentance first to God and then to you. Forgiveness is not a feeling; it is a choice you make. Once forgiveness has been chosen, the road back to trust is long and difficult. It is important for you to pray and think about specific ways your husband can demonstrate to you that he is serious about rebuilding the trust. Part of that process should include you asking your husband at any time of the day how he is doing with his sobriety—his abstinence from pornography.

18. Appeal to your husband on the basis of your children.

You both love your children (if you have them). Appeal to your husband on the basis of your children. Ask him to consider the damage his pornography viewing will do to them, not only if they find it and see it, but the inevitable pain it will cause them to have a father who is emotionally distant, spiritually absent, and unable to be a godly father training your children in the way they should go. Ask your husband: "Would you want someone looking at our daughter the way you looked at someone else's daughter in pornography?" Pose this question to him, "Do you want our children to struggle with pornography like you are struggling?" Porn harms women and children. No man's Christianity could ever affirm contributing to that harm.

19. Encourage him to take the 1 Million Men Living a Pornography-Free Life Challenge.

Go to the commitment section of Join1MillionMen.org, and ask him to make the commitment from this day forward to live a pornography-free life. Get a copy of *Our Hardcore Battle Plan A–Z* and have your husband read it. Then discuss it together. Ask him to go to Join1MillionMen.org, and to get on the wall where men publicly commit to be porn-free.

20. Communicate with your husband your needs each day.

There will be days when you feel you are making progress and other days where the enemy attacks you emotionally and spiritually. It is vitally important that you communicate with your husband exactly how you are feeling and what you are thinking, especially early in the discovery of his pornography habit.

21. Be your husband's number one prayer warrior.

Let him know you are his biggest intercessor, that you will be doing battle for him in prayer and taking him before the throne of God multiple times during the day. There are days you won't want to pray for him because of the pain he has caused you; however, push through the pain and pray anyway! God will honor that.

22. Pray for his protection daily—spiritually, physically, emotionally, and mentally.

Do battle for the heart and mind of your husband. You are in a battle for his relationship with Christ, his life, for your marriage, for the father of your children. Like Job, pray that God would build walls of protection around him (Job 1:10). However you must know that you cannot be responsible for his pornography struggle. That is his choice. He alone has to answer to God for what he does.

In praying for her husband, Greg, who was addicted to pornography and having an affair, Cathy Dyer said:

> I could pray for him, and I realized that I was one of his best advocates because I knew him better than others. We are called as wives to be a helpmate to our husband, and daily prayer is a major part of that. We have access to the throne of God—why not use that access to ask for a hedge of protection around our husband's mind and eyes and to ask for strength in the midst of temptation?

23. You can't "fix" your husband's struggle with pornography.

He alone has to choose to say yes to purity and no to porn. It is important to understand that God can bring freedom to your husband, but you cannot. You can encourage him, pray for him, affirm him, love him, provide for his physical needs, but you cannot be responsible for his choice to look at pornography. Refuse to allow your husband to blame, justify, or rationalize his looking at porn. He has to have a plan and a process to break free and he must daily work at it. Memorizing verses such as these can help: "I can do all things through Him who strengthens me" (Philippians 4:13). "Now to Him who is able to do far more abundantly beyond all that we ask or think, according to the power that works within us" (Ephesians 3:20).

24. **Your Christian husband can overcome in his battle with pornography but not without a passionate commitment to purity.**

When his desire to be a godly man is greater than his desire to look at pornography, then and only then will living a pornography-free life become a reality.

If your husband makes the choice to continue looking at pornography, you have the freedom, for your sake and the sake of your children, to remove yourself from that atmosphere. Your husband must make a choice: either you or pornography, his family or pornography, God or pornography. You cannot be responsible for his sinful choices. If he chooses pornography, a separation with the hopes of his repentance and healing could be necessary. Hang on to God's promise that: "with God all things are possible" (Matthew 19:26).

25. **Make it a personal mission to bring this issue of pornography to your pastor and church.**

The majority of pastors are simply not addressing the issue of Christian men struggling with pornography. Ask your pastor to challenge the men in the church to take the hardcore challenge and join 1 million men in churches of all sizes and denominations in living pornography free. Behind every great movement that has changed our communities, nation, and world, and has had an impact on our churches, there have been godly women who prayed and got proactive. You can change things! Do what you can to make sure your church is silent no more on this subject.

26. **God has given you a story! Use it!**

The process you have gone through is extremely painful. There is a wound in your soul. You feel insecure, angry, betrayed, and lonely. As you turn to your heavenly Father and cry out to Him, healing will come, not overnight, but it will come as you continue seeking Him. Regardless of whether your husband repents, God has given you a story through what has happened. God never wastes our sorrows and pain. As you experience healing, God will bring other hurting souls into your life, who are facing the same thing with their husbands. Through your difficult test, God has given you a testimony that can cause you and others to be overcomers.

> *All praise to God, the Father of our Lord Jesus Christ. God is our merciful Father and the source of all comfort. He comforts us in all our troubles so that we can comfort others. When they are troubled, we will be able to give them the same comfort God has given us.*
>
> —2 Corinthians 1:3–4 (NLT)

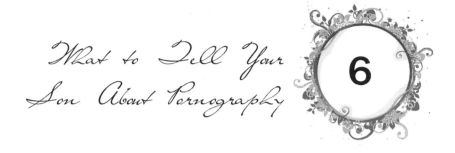

What to Tell Your Son About Pornography

6

As a parent, there are issues that are awkward to address. Sex is certainly one of those difficult issues. When you include pornography in the discussion, it could be even more uncomfortable.

In our biblical job description of *parent*, we are to encourage, train, direct, counsel, warn, and explain. We know that more than 90 percent of teenagers have been exposed to pornography (many times by accident and not intentionally). They are also being bombarded with sexualized messages daily at school, through media, and messaging. This letter provides a tool you and your husband can use to communicate the dangers of pornography to your child. I encourage you to pray over this letter. Ask God to give you wisdom to know when to share it. Ask your son to read it, and then set a specific time to discuss it.

Dear Son:

You are living in an exciting time in history in which technology is exploding with possibilities. What was unthinkable just a few years ago is now possible, primarily because of the Internet. With social media part of your everyday life, a big world becomes much smaller. Who knows what is coming in the next few years? You can't even imagine living in a world without mobile phones or devices, tablets, social media, Web sites, and texting. I am happy that you are alive at a time when knowledge is literally at your fingertips.

But, with these technological advances comes a danger that is as real as anything ever created. Lurking behind every portal online, on television, and on your cell phone, there is something that is calling your name and inviting you to click the mouse, change the channel, or use your phone to access an image, a picture, or a scene.

That danger is pornography—sexual images that invite you to watch something that will harm you and has the potential to destroy everything that is important in your life. Once you open the door to pornography, it will do its damage. It leaves memories that you wish you did not have. Porn will encourage thoughts that cannot be acted on in a way that pleases God. Simply put, there is nothing good that comes from viewing pornography—nothing!

Pornography lies to you! It lies as it says:

1. Women exist to bring pleasure to men.
2. Women don't have emotions and needs.
3. You'll never have any consequences from acting on what you see in pornography.
4. Lusting after someone is normal and acceptable.
5. Sex is only a physical act.
6. Sex is the number one need in your life.
7. Pornography is normal.
8. Oral sex is not sex.
9. You don't have to wait until you are married to have sex.
10. You aren't physically able to wait to have sex until you are married.

Lies enslave you. God always tells you the truth, and acting on God's truth will allow you to live in wonderful freedom and joy instead of being a slave.

My prayer is that if you have seen pornography, you will choose with God's help to never look at it again. I know the pressure comes from both inside of you and forces outside of you trying to get you to look. The world, without God, has made it very easy for you to see pornography. Only with God's power will you get victory. You will have to fight hard spiritually to claim Psalm 101:3 (NLT): "I will refuse to look at anything vile and vulgar." The Message paraphrase puts it this way: "I refuse to take a second look at corrupting people and degrading things."

Recently a study was conducted on the activity of the brain and specifically one's thoughts. It has been established that the time between when a thought hits your mind and your acting on that thought is one-quarter of a second! That's certainly not very much time, but it is enough if you allow God to be in control. You will have strong temptations, even the temptation to look at pornography; however, you can train your mind to confess your sinful thought, replace that thought with God's truth from the Bible, and not act on the thought.

As your parent I won't always be there to warn you or to encourage you. But God is very real and He has promised to always give you the power to say yes to what is right and no to what is wrong.

If someone came to you and told you that a bottle of poison was really candy, would it still poison you? Yes! If someone told you that fire didn't burn, would it still burn if you touched it? Of course it would! As your parent, what I am saying to you is that pornography is a poison that will destroy everything good. It is a fire that will burn you and leave scars. It is a minefield that will destroy God's good plans for you.

Son, if you have viewed pornography, there is no way to undo what you have seen. That image is permanently etched on your memory. So what do you do? First, it's what you don't do, and that is intentionally looking at pornography. Secondly, you confess that you have had sinful thoughts. Thirdly, replace those thoughts with biblical truth. That's why it is important to read the Bible daily and get God's perspective.

God has the most wonderful plan for you when it comes to sex. God is telling you the truth. Satan and those who leave God out of their lives and their thinking are not telling you the truth.

Son, I want God's very best for you and the best He has for you does not include pornography. I am asking you to make a commitment right now to God and to me that from this day forward you will be committed to living a porn-free life. If you do, you will experience a freedom and happiness you could not believe.

Son, I love you and want you to always know I am here for you anytime. Although discussing sexual issues can be awkward, I want you to know that I am available to talk with you, listen to you, and pray with you. I commit for as long as I live to pray daily for you that you will always choose to follow God's way. Pornography is never God's way.

Blessings,
Your Name(s) here

When Women Are Addicted to Pornography

7

Lust and sexual sin have no gender. Lust never asks, "Are you male or female?"

—covenanteyes.com

At covenanteyes.com, the title of Jessica Harris's blog caught my attention: "Porn Is a Co-Ed Sin."

I believe that Christian men, upwards of 80 percent of them, are struggling with viewing pornography at some level. However, Christian women are struggling, too, not yet to the degree men are struggling, but the percentages are continually increasing.

Even more than Christian men, Christian women are struggling in silence and living in quiet shame. Younger women are taking on more of the characteristics of the male in that they are being visually stimulated.

Viewing pornography is not just a "guy thing." Although the outcome of lust is destruction, for males and females there are some distinctions in the motivation and process of becoming involved in pornography.

The problem of women and specifically Christian women being involved in pornography will continue to increase. Summarizing the runaway best-selling trilogy, "Fifty Shades," one article said:

> *Fifty Shades of Grey* has topped best-seller lists around the world, including the United Kingdom and the United States. The series has sold over 65 million copies worldwide, with book rights having been sold in 37 countries, and set the record as

the fastest-selling paperback of all time, selling even faster than the *Harry Potter* series in paperback.

Sadly, *Fifty Shades of Grey* is being read by many Christian women too. The popularity of this book tells us that women are struggling as never before. Frank Santos of the *New York Daily News* said: "*Fifty Shades of Grey* is pornography, plain and simple. It's a kind of pornography that attracts only women and thus far it is selling off the charts."

What Is the Difference Between Men and Women Concerning Pornography?

This is not meant to be an oversimplification, but in general, men are looking for a release sexually and women are searching for a personal connection, a relationship. Pornography for women becomes a step toward that connection. For men, pornography is an end in itself, usually ending with acting out sexually (through masturbation). For women, pornography is usually not an end in itself but a means to a relationship, a means to an emotional connection, which often involves a real-life connection. Some women are viewing pornography in an attempt to discover what they need to do to please men, and get the attention and affection they desire.

We simply can no longer ignore the fact that pornography viewing is a problem for women too—even Christian women. Churches and Christian leaders have to begin to address this subject. Yes, it is sensitive and at times embarrassing to discuss, but an entire generation of women depend upon the church to give validity to their struggle. The following statistics open the door to let us see the feminine side of the world of pornography:

• Women make up 30 percent of Internet pornography viewers.
• Seventeen percent of women struggle with pornography addiction.
• Ratio of women to men favoring chat rooms—2-to-1
• Percentages of visitors to adult Web sites who are women—1 in 3 visitors
• Women admitting to accessing pornography at work—23 percent

- Women, far more than men, are likely to act out their behaviors in real life, such as having multiple partners, casual sex, or affairs, according to Internet Filter Review.

- Currently, about 25 percent of Christian women are addicted to pornography, 70 percent of whom will never confess it, blogs "Dirty Girls Come Clean," an online support system for women who struggle with lustful behaviors.

- Thirty-four percent of readers of *Today's Christian Woman's* online newsletter admitted to intentionally accessing Internet porn.

- Though 70 percent of women say they keep their online viewing habits secret, there's no question that more and more women are watching and buying erotica and porn, according to a report by Lisa Ling on "Adult Films, Porn, and Erotica."

In a *Today's Christian Woman* blog, *Women and Porn*, Marnie Ferree, a licensed marriage and family therapist, wrote an article on addictions. She is a former sex addict and director of Bethesda Workshops, an organization that offers faith-based, clinical, intensive treatment for sexual addiction and coaddiction. In the article, "Women Struggle, Too (with Sexual Addiction)," she suggests that "one-third of sex addicts are women, and eventual information will reveal women comprise nearly one-half of those who are sexually addicted." Ferree reports that:

> A growing number of women are looking online at the more traditional kind of pornography. Generally speaking, most women who choose visual material are younger females, ages 18–34. This generation was raised in a media-saturated culture and is more accustomed to visual stimuli. Advances in neuroscience indicate that our media-driven culture is literally altering the human brain—and not just men's. Today's young women seem equally visually oriented. It is no surprise, then, that females are drawn to pornographic pictures.

According to a study cited by ABC, about 78 percent of women porn addicts were sexually abused or neglected and experienced a lack of emotional support from their families.

A number of studies among college-age women are very telling:

- Coming from adolescence into adulthood, nearly half of women today believe viewing pornography is acceptable behavior.

- According to a survey of more than 11,000 young women, more than half of young women today are exposed to sexually explicit material by the age of 14.

- By the age of 18, more than 60 percent of women have seen pornography.

- Nearly a third of young adult women intentionally use pornography from time to time.

- About 1 in 5 women (18 percent) watch porn habitually—every week

—covenanteyes.com

William Struthers writes in *Wired for Intimacy: How Pornography Hijacks the Male Brain*:

The female brain, unlike the male brain, is wired to understand sexual arousal first as "contextual" and then as "sensory." What this means is when a young woman looks at porn, [her] brain learns what it means to be wanted by a man. When women see porn, any attraction to it initially is to think, "This is what guys want, so this is what I should become." For women, their initial curiosity about porn is usually to imagine themselves as the wanted party. Only after this do women become visually aroused by pornography images themselves.

However, a shift is taking place today as more and more women are exposed to pornography at younger ages. Struthers says research indicates women over the age of 35 are much less likely to develop habitual, compulsive, impulsive, or addictive pornography viewing habits when compared to women under the age of 35. The reason is because the younger a woman is, her brain is more able to be trained and taught to interpret the anxiety she feels as sexual tension, and so women "are becoming increasingly more likely to view pornography and to develop maladaptive or compulsive patterns of viewing and sexually acting out as well."

In a recent survey of the online community of Dirty Girls Ministries, 95 percent of those surveyed said they started habitually and compulsively watching pornography or engaging in cybersex before the age of 30.

Beyond every statistic and reference we can provide, women themselves know whether or not they are struggling with pornography. It's no secret to them.

What is a Christian woman to do?

Whether you are struggling personally with pornography and lust or a friend is struggling, here are ten specific steps to bring freedom from the chains of lust:

1. Surrender your lust to God.

Admit the struggle of lust and surrender it to God. He has the power to break the chains of bondage. Your lust is not too strong for the power of our resurrected Savior. No more excuses. No more blaming. No more justifying. No more secrets. With a heart of brokenness, go to our grace-giving Father and admit, "This is bigger than me, but not bigger than You." Trust Him to give you the power to break free. You need the Father's forgiveness and He is willing to give it, no matter what you have looked at or done.

Enough is enough and it's time to come clean. Surrender your lustful acts and perverse thoughts to God. Surrender your sinful relationships to God. Surrender your addiction to sexually-explicit television programs and movies to God. Surrender reading inappropriate books and Web sites to God.

The first step is an act of absolute surrender; all the ugly stuff must be taken to the Cross with a heart of brokenness and humility. Personally claim these Scriptures:

Psalm 9:10: *And those who know Your name will put their trust in You, for You, O Lord, have not forsaken those who seek You.*

Romans 12:1: *Therefore I urge you, brethren, by the mercies of God, to present your bodies a living and holy sacrifice, acceptable to God, which is your spiritual service of worship.*

James 4:8: *Draw near to God and He will draw near to you. Cleanse your hands, you sinners; and purify your hearts, you double-minded.*

Isaiah 55:6–7: *Seek the Lord while He may be found; call upon Him while He is near. Let the wicked forsake his way and the unrighteous man his thoughts; and let him return to the Lord; and He will have compassion on him.*

Confess to Him, "God, I am afraid." "God, I am embarrassed." "God, I am ashamed." He loves you no matter what you have done, but the Holy Spirit will not allow you as a believer to stay where you are without convicting you and giving you every opportunity to become free.

Dietrich Bonhoeffer, in *Disciplines of a Godly Man*, made the observation that when lust takes control, "At this moment God . . . loses all reality. . . . Satan does not fill us with hatred of God, but with forgetfulness of God." What a world of wisdom there is in this statement! When we are in the grip of lust, the reality of God fades. This is what lust does! It has done it millions of times.

2. Search for the answer to the question, "Why is lust a problem for me?"

There is a reason lust is a problem in your life. Think about what is driving that desire for sexual gratification outside of God's will. Getting to the source of the problem is necessary for living in freedom not only today but the rest of your life.

Crystal Renaud, as a young woman, was addicted to pornography. The 26-year-old shared her intimate journey from addiction in her book *Dirty Girls Come Clean*. She wrote:

> What's important to know about pornography and sexual addiction as a whole is that it's almost never about sex. It's a core intimacy disorder. Core wounds that have gone unhealed and are being medicated in the wrong way. We see women all the time addicted to pornography simply because they are using it as a way to cope with pain in their lives.

Consider some of the reasons you may be struggling with lust and pornography. That doesn't excuse it, but it does help you to understand some of the underlying motivations:
• You were abandoned or abused by a parent or authority figure.
• You have a strained or broken relationship with your husband.
• You had an early exposure to pornography.
• You were sexually abused as a child.
• You have unmet emotional needs.
• You experience a lack of affection from your husband.
• You have a need for attention or affirmation from men.
• You experienced a past trauma.
• You are influenced by an ungodly friend.
• You have been exposed to sexualized media.
• You read erotic romance novels.

• You have unclear boundaries when dealing with men.

• You have been talking about your marriage problems with another man.

If you see yourself in this list, now is the time to pull back the layers of hurt and reveal your wounds for healing through the light of God's Word and God's love. You cannot do this alone; you need others to help you, other women who have walked this path and experienced freedom; other women who have been trained to help you, to give you the tools you need to get healthy; other women who are God-centered, prayer-focused, and grace-oriented.

3. Satan's two big lies must be rejected now!

Satan is a real enemy whose power rests in his lies. He attempts to convince you that you cannot change and break free. Live in the reality of John 8:44 and John 8:32:

> *You are of your father the devil, and you want to do the desires of your father. He was a murderer from the beginning, and does not stand in the truth because there is no truth in him. Whenever he speaks a lie, he speaks from his own nature, for he is a liar and the father of lies.*
>
> — John 8:44

> *And you will know the truth, and the truth will make you free.*
>
> —John 8:32

Lie Number 1

Everyone does it.

Satan wants you to believe that there is absolutely nothing wrong with what you are doing. He whispers that this is the twenty-first century and this is just a natural feeling and curiosity, that there's no harm in reading *Fifty Shades of Grey*, looking at pornography, getting in a chat room, or going to a strip club. *Girls just want to have fun!* Satan will attempt to minimize the sin of lust as acceptable. We know that God says just the opposite.

Lie Number 2
You are the only one who struggles.
Satan wants you to believe that no other Christian woman struggles with lust and pornography—only you. That sense of aloneness and shame keeps driving you deeper into despair. He wants you to believe that if other people knew of your struggle they wouldn't love you anymore; they would think you are some kind of freak of nature. Again, this is a lie from our enemy.

4. Seek God's forgiveness through repentance.
Without repentance, nothing ever changes. Repentance involves brokenness. It is a moment in which God, the Holy Spirit, convicts you to truly change the direction you are going. You recognize your sin as being destructive in your life and contrary to God's will. You experience an overwhelming sense of sorrow for what you have done. You vow, in God's power, to no longer do what God has revealed as sin in your life. Where there is no change, there has been no repentance. The process of repentance involves:

> RECOGNITION—You have an acute awareness that you have sinned.

> RESPONSIBILITY—You blame no one else for your choices and actions.

> RELEASE—You confess your specific sin(s) to God.

> REQUEST—You ask God to forgive you.

> REMOVE—You must distance yourself from that which causes you to fall into sin.

RETURN—You once again strive to do only the will of God.

REJOICE—You can know victory and freedom from sin and guilt. By faith claim God's forgiveness.

5. Sources of pornography and lust must be eliminated.

Whatever the source of your pornography, immediately destroy it. Cut off any sinful relationship. Get out of any chat room. Cut off relationships that encourage a casual approach to sexual issues.

Paul said, "Bad company corrupts good morals" (1 Corinthians 15:33). If necessary, destroy your computer. The reminders of past experiences on that computer may be too hard to overcome. Remove premium cable from your television. Avoid reality television shows that glamorize affairs, pornography, or sex outside of marriage. Throw away erotic novels. Seriously evaluate your time spent in social media. That may be a source of temptation for you.

6. Share your struggle with a godly, trusted friend.

Who is the godliest woman you know? Who can you trust? It is absolutely essential to share this with another woman. A secret possesses chaining power. Once you reveal the secret to another person, that secret begins to lose its power over you. "Therefore, confess your sins to one another, and pray for one another so that you may be healed" (James 5:16).

Initially that woman may be a Christian counselor, trained to help give you tools for overcoming. Think about an older, godly woman who could be your mentor, helping you to stay on track spiritually.

7. Sit down with your husband and tell him your struggle.

You must get honest with your husband. Keeping your struggle with pornography a secret from him will be used by Satan to keep you in bondage.

This is a painful but necessary step you must take. An idea for sharing with your husband: write down your thoughts in the form of a letter, thinking through every word, communicating your grief, and expressing your true repentance and sorrow for what you have done to him. Once you have written your letter, pray over it, and ask God to help you share it. Ask God to prepare your husband's heart to hear what you are going to share. At an appropriate time (but as soon as possible), in a quiet place with no distractions, read the letter to him.

8. Spiritual disciplines are essential to remain pure.

First Timothy 4:7 says, "Discipline yourself for the purpose of godliness." Donald Whitney writes, in *Spiritual Disciplines for the Christian Life*:

> The spiritual disciplines are those personal and corporate disciplines that promote spiritual growth. They are the habits of devotion and experiential Christianity that have been practiced by the people of God since biblical times. . . . The Spiritual Disciplines are the God-given means we are to use in the Spirit-filled pursuit of Godliness

There are essential spiritual disciplines that need to become habits in your life. Read the Bible daily. Meditate on Scripture. Take one verse a day and read it, reflect on it, pray it, and then ask the Holy Spirit to speak to you through that Scripture. Have a set time to pray but also pray throughout the day. Worship the Lord by praising Him for Who He is and what He has done. Have a set time each day where you have solitude, an opportunity to be still and experience God's presence. Journal: write down what God is saying to you and what you are saying to God. As God leads you, practice fasting, going without so you can seek God more intensely.

9. Support groups are healing communities. Get in one!

You experience healing in a healing community. You cannot get free by yourself. A support group for encouragement, accountability, and prayer cannot be overemphasized. Find a support group that addresses female sexual addictions. Look to your church or a Bible-centered church where you live. Check out these Web sites to assist you with this:

- Freedomeveryday.org
- Faithfulandtrueministries.com
- Purelifeministries.com
- Bethesdaworkshops.org
- Celebraterecovery.com

10. Set specific and clear boundaries in relationships with men.

Draw some very specific, clear, and unbreakable boundaries in relationship to men other than your husband. In our sexualized culture where the majority of men are viewing pornography, many are viewing you as a sexual object. Even the godliest of men have struggles with lust. Let me offer some guidelines:

Never travel alone with another man—never!

Never flirt with a man who is not your husband.

Cease emailing or texting personal things to other men.

Never talk with another man about the problems you have in your marriage.

Never give another man your personal information. You cannot be best friends with a man who is not your husband.

If there is a man where you work, who is tempting you or is attempting to flirt with you, through your actions, attitudes, and demeanor, show that you will not "go there." Take any action necessary to prevent further conversations.

Do not contact an ex-boyfriend, ex-husband, or any man with whom you had a former relationship.

If you are living with someone not your husband, stop living together until you either get married, or determine that this man is not God's will for your life.

Do not make connections with men on Facebook or other social media outlets. This is not being unfriendly; you are just guarding your heart.

My former assistant, Bonnie Hicks, who walked through the pain of her husband's pornography addiction and infidelity, has counseled many women. One thing Bonnie shares is, "Don't live another day wanting to change!" You don't have to *want to* change; you *can* change when you choose to do things God's way.

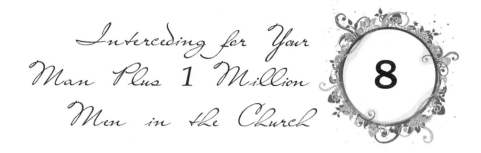

Interceding for Your Man Plus 1 Million Men in the Church

8

The following are examples of specific prayers you can pray as a wife, mother, and church member for your husband, son, and men in churches. There is great power in intercession. Whether your husband, or son, or other family member is struggling with pornography, your prayers can change things. Your prayers for the husbands of your friends or their sons will make a difference. Also your prayers for the men in the church you attend or men in all churches can have a transforming effect.

It is my conviction that the number one reason revival is being hindered in churches is the impurity in the lives of Christian men due to their habit of viewing pornography. Throughout history the prayers of godly women have been the catalyst for revival. Behind every great movement that has changed our country and impacted our churches, there have been godly women who prayed and got proactive. You can change things. There is no circumstance so dark and no situation so hopeless that God cannot break through and bring hope, healing, and *hallelujahs*!

Scriptural Prayer Promises

Pray without ceasing (1 Thessalonians 5:17).

This is the confidence which we have before Him that, if we ask anything according to His will, He hears us. And if we know that He hears us in whatever we ask, we know that we have the requests which we have asked from Him (1 John 5:14–15).

Ask and it will be given to you; seek and you will find; knock and it will be opened to you. For everyone who asks receives, and he who seeks finds, and to him who knocks it will be opened (Matthew 7:7–8).

Truly I say to you, whatever you bind on earth shall have been bound in heaven; and whatever you loose on earth shall have been loosed in heaven. Again I say to you, that if two of you agree on earth about anything that they may ask, it shall be done for them by My Father who is in heaven (Matthew 18:18–19).

And all things you ask in prayer, believing, you will receive (Matthew 21:22).

And He said to them, "This kind cannot come out by anything but prayer" (Mark 9:29).

Therefore I say to you, all things for which you pray and ask, believe that you have received them, and they will be granted you (Mark 11:24).

Whatever you ask in My name, that will I do, so that the Father may be glorified in the Son. If you ask Me anything in My name, I will do it (John 14:13–14).

Now to Him who is able to do far more abundantly beyond all that we ask or think, according to the power that works within us (Ephesians 3:20).

With all prayer and petition pray at all times in the Spirit, and with this in view, be on the alert with all perseverance and petition for all the saints (Ephesians 6:18).

In my distress I called upon the Lord, And cried to my God for help; He heard my voice out of His temple, and my cry for help before Him came into His ears (Psalm 18:6).

He will call upon Me, and I will answer him; I will be with him in trouble; I will rescue him and honor him (Psalm 91:15).

From my distress I called upon the Lord; The Lord answered me and set me in a large place (Psalm 118:5).

So I gave my attention to the Lord God to seek Him by prayer and supplications, with fasting, sackcloth and ashes (Daniel 9:3).

Is anyone among you sick? Let them call the elders of the church to pray over them and anoint them with oil in the name of the Lord. And the prayer offered in faith will make the sick person well; the Lord will raise them up. If they have sinned, they will be forgiven. Therefore confess your sins to each other and pray for each other so that you may be healed. The prayer of a righteous person is powerful and effective? (James 5:14–16 NIV).

Prayer Quotes

"We need to agonize as well as organize."

—John Blanchard

"Prayer is the sweat of the soul."

—Martin Luther

"Prayer is the language of a man burdened with a sense of need."

—E. M. Bounds

"God tells us to burden Him with whatever burdens us."

—Anonymous

"Time spent in prayer is never wasted."

— Francois Fenelon

"You can do more than pray after you have prayed, but you cannot do more than pray until you have prayed."

—S. D. Gordon

"Restraining prayer we cease to fight;
prayer makes the Christian's armour bright;
and Satan trembles when he sees,
the weakest saint upon his knees."

—William Cowper

"When I pray coincidences happen, and when I do not, they don't."

—William Temple

"God loves to be consulted."

—Charles Bridges

"Turn the Bible into prayer."

—Robert Murray McCheyne

"Prayer is receiving what God has promised."

—E. F. Hallock

"To effectively combat the devil, you need to pray."

—Pedro Okoro

"Men may spurn our appeals, reject our message, oppose our arguments, despise our persons, but they are helpless against our prayers."

—J. Sidlow Baxter

Prayer of a Wife for Her Husband

Dear God:

Today I am praying for my husband, asking You to help him to have a passion for purity. I know there is a daily assault upon his eyes and his mind and that pornography will attempt to find its way into his life. Please protect him from that and protect him from allowing sinful thoughts and fantasies to remain in his mind even for one second. Protect him from temptations that are designed to attack his purity. Help him to keep his eyes on You and to experience power through surrender to You. Show him how to guard his heart. Please help him to be aware of Satan's traps and temptations. May my husband daily seek You through reading the Bible. Help him to be a man of prayer and character. Direct his every step today and help him to confess sinful thoughts immediately and replace them with Your Word. Give me daily insight on how to encourage my husband toward purity in mind, body, and emotions.

In Jesus' name, amen.

Prayer of a Mother for Her Son

Dear God:

Today I am praying for my son, asking You to protect him from pornography and the chains that viewing it brings. I realize my son's mind is being intentionally targeted by the pornography industry in an effort to tempt him and trap him into viewing it. Please help him protect his eyes and his mind from pornographic images, and give him a passion to seek purity. I pray

Your hedge of protection around him. I pray for godly influences to surround him and I pray against wrong influences from entering his life. Give me the knowledge I need to protect my son from pornography and the wisdom to know if he is struggling with this issue. Please break any bondage that is confronting my son, in Jesus' name. I plead the blood of Jesus over my son and his future so that he would become a man of passionate purity. I pray for his future wife, that you will keep her pure and protect her from the consequences of other men viewing pornography.

I pray in Jesus' name, amen.

Prayer of Women for Men in Churches

God of the impossible:

Today I am asking You for something great for men in the churches. I pray for at least 1 million men to make a commitment to live a porn-free life. I pray for pastors and Christian leaders to set the example and to communicate the need for purity among men in the church. Guard them from the poison of pornography. I pray for the wives of the men who are struggling with pornography, that you would give them discernment, wisdom, and strength to confront and deal with this problem. Give them grace and firmness in addressing this issue with their husbands. Please help my church to address the tide of pornography that is plaguing our men. I also pray You will raise up godly men to challenge other men in the church to live porn-free lives. I cry out to You, God, for a revival of purity among men in the church.

I pray in Jesus' name, amen.

Making a Commitment to Pray for 1 Million Men

You can make a difference in the lives of men in churches all over the United States and the world. God has used the prayers of women throughout all ages to change the course of history. Legendary nineteen-century missionary to China, Hudson Taylor, said, "It is possible to move men, through God, by prayer alone."

A revival of purity among men in the church could change our world. I believe you, through prayer, could move at least one million men to live a pornography-free life. I am asking for you to be one of 1 million women praying for one million men. Would you make a commitment to do the following?

❏ Commit to pray for at least 1 million men in churches to become pornography free. Ask the Holy Spirit to:

❏ Convict men in the church to live a pornography-free life.

❏ Help men understand the threat of pornography to their intimacy with God, their marriages, families, and Christian leadership.

❏ Burden men in the church to reach out to other men in accountability relationships, encouraging them to live pornography-free lives.

❏ Commit to pray for pastors and Christian leaders in churches to feel a burden to address the issue of pornography with boldness and conviction.

❏ Communicate with your Christian women friends about the need to pray for 1 million men in churches to become pornography-free.

❏ Pray for a hedge of protection around the minds and hearts of boys and teenage males in churches that they will choose to live pornography-free lives.

AFTERWORD:

To Live Free

Years ago God placed a burden on my heart for this exciting, God-sized project to create the content and campaign for 1 million Christian men to say, "I will take Jesus seriously when He said, "*The pure in heart will see God*" (Matthew 5:8).

For men to see God work in their lives, their marriages, and families, their hearts must be pure. And the heart cannot be pure if pornography is part of a man's (or woman's) life.

The good news is that when a man allows the Holy Spirit to preside within him, freedom can be attained and maintained. I've seen it happen and so has Cathy, as she has described in this book.

I pray that you'll use the information you've found here to help break the bonds that pornography may have on those you know, and on those you love. And I hope that you will be moved to place your name on the women's virtual prayer wall on Join1MillionMen.org to become one of 1 million women praying for 1 million men to be pornography free.

For all who struggle: Truth will set you free, and living in truth and grace will keep you free.

A young man and a father of two boys share their commitment to Join 1 Million Men

My Journal

Date _____

My Journal

Date _____

My Journal

Date _____

My Journal

Date _____

My Journal

Date _____

My Journal

Date _____

My Journal

Date _____

My Journal

Date _____

My Journal

Date _____

My Journal

Date _____

New Hope® Publishers is a division of WMU®, an international organization that challenges Christian believers to understand and be radically involved in God's mission. For more information about WMU, go to wmu.com. More information about New Hope books may be found at NewHopeDigital.com. New Hope books may be purchased at your local bookstore.

Use the QR reader on your
smartphone to visit us online at
NewHopeDigital.com

If you've been blessed by this book, we would like to hear your story.
The publisher and author welcome your comments and
suggestions at: newhopereader@wmu.org.

Our Hardcore Battle Plan:
1 Million Women Praying

JOIN
1 MILLION
MEN

Be 1 woman in the growing sisterhood committing to pray for the men in our lives committing to live porn-free. Our Hardcore Battle Plan: 1 Million Women Praying gives women 26 key Scriptures for prayer and reflection, and practical tips and tools for helping the men we love to keep pornography out of their lives. In this simple A-Z format, you'll be encouraged to pass this along as a prayer guide and encourage other women to join

**1 Million Women Praying
in the war against pornography!**

You can find the 1 Million Women Praying prayer booklet at Join1MillionMen.org in addition to other helpful resources in the "Join 1 Million Men in the War Against Pornography" series.

NEW HOPE
PUBLISHERS
Gospel-Centered. Missions-Driven.

WMU
missions for life